DRESS LIKE THE BIG FISH

How to Achieve the Image You Want and the Success You Deserve

Dick Lerner, CWC, CCC

Bel Air Fashions Press, Inc.
Omaha, Nebraska

Bel Air Fashions Press, Inc.
717 North 114th Street
Omaha, NE 68154
www.DressLikeTheBigFish.com

Cataloging in Publication on File with Publisher

Library of Congress Cataloging Number 2007928552
ISBN13: 978-0-9793463-0-9
ISBN10: 0-9793463-0-4

Printed in the U.S.A.

10 9 8 7 6 5 4 3 2

Acknowledgments

To my wonderful wife and best friend, Martha, and my kids Ali, Mark, Brad and Jon – for all their input and support.

For my lifelong brother and partner, Shelly, who puts up with more than anyone. It's what we have accomplished in business that makes this book possible.

Also to Glenn Davis, retired Nebraska Director of the SBA, for his close friendship and expertise. He has been my sounding board.

To Lisa Pelto of Concierge Marketing Inc. and her team for bringing this book to life!

To Howard Epstein, longtime friend and attorney, for helping with the filings and paperwork.

To our wonderful clients for their kind words and encouragement.

Contents

Foreword

Years ago, after over 13 years in the Air Force, I found myself transitioning from flying jets for the Air Force to becoming self-employed as an author and presenter in the civilian world. Being stationed in nearby Omaha, Nebraska, I had heard of the dedication of Richard Lerner and his brother Shelly of Bel Air Fashions. I so needed help. These two gentlemen were kind enough to spend hours helping me to understand color, fabrics, construction and fit of a gentleman's wardrobe. They made it easy. Through their efforts, I was able to mix-and-match, dress up or down fitting for any occasion. I'm proud to say that when I met President Reagan, I was dressed entirely through Bel Air Fashions. Whether I'm on "Oprah," speaking with Fortune 500 companies or young adults, Richard and Shelly are with me every step of the way. If you are looking for a book that makes getting dressed easy – then this is the book for you.

David Pelzer, author of *A Child Called "IT"*
#1 New York Times Best Selling Author
2006 National Jefferson Award Recipient

Introduction

Why did you buy that sport coat at the mall? Did you absolutely have to have the brown leather handbag? Does that tie with the stripes go with anything else in your closet?

Ever give clothing away that has never been worn? Did that make you sick? It's like burning dollar bills in the fireplace and watching the ashes rise and disappear.

Buying and wearing clothes doesn't have to be that way. With the information in this book, you will never buy clothing again without a reason. You can buy garments that pay you a return on your investment. You can have a wardrobe that pays dividends over and over throughout the year, and you'll have the flexibility of a year-round wardrobe that you can dress up or down on a moment's notice.

Wouldn't it be nice to be dressed for any situation that people will take notice?

Men and women buy clothing for many reasons. You buy clothing and accessories for many different reasons. Maybe you prefer a certain name brand or designer or because something you like is on sale. If you fill your closet with no direction or purpose in mind, that's an expensive way to build a wardrobe. Buy clothing with a specific purpose in mind.

The purpose of this book is to help you plan your wardrobe before you buy. In the long run it is the least expensive way to build a winning wardrobe. Clothing that has a reason to go in the closet will coordinate with other garments that you have.

This book will help you know what to wear and when to wear it. Wardrobes that can be dressed up, dressed down and mixed-and-matched on a moment's notice can have a huge return on investment – in you and your career. Never base your clothing buys on a designer or name brand label. Sale merchandise is fine as long as it fits into your wardrobe – and is not left hanging in the back of the closet. The unplanned purchase, more than likely, is never worn, doesn't go with anything and is often discarded with the sale tags still attached.

Purchasing a well-defined wardrobe is based on fabric, color, construction, fit and models that work for you, not on sale price or label. Planning your wardrobe according to your daily activities and lifestyle will determine what you accumulate and what goes to charity today.

Personal appearance is just as important as your clothing. Grooming, personal hygiene, hairstyle, cosmetics, and fragrances, along with clothing, are nonverbal messages and impressions we convey to other people. Clothing and non-clothing items define you and create those critical first impressions. Together they shape the image you project.

This book takes you through the steps toward career success. You'll learn how personal appearance makes a key difference, how your image can be controlled and how to make a winning first impression. You'll find out what to wear to an interview so you look as polished as your resume.

Then we'll look at clothing that helps you transition from the interview to your career. You'll find out what to wear – whether it's professional, business casual or casual – and your closet will be prepared, too. Not knowing what to wear is like being a fish out of water. Knowing the difference will help you dress like the big fish you hope to become.

This book will also help you understand how important accessories are to your overall image and first impression. If you are going to take the time to prepare, make sure your image is complete and that the details are well thought out.

I have conducted many workshops over the years and am often asked, "Where can I find the wardrobe and image information I discuss?" Until now, nowhere. That's why I am writing this book. It's an easy-to-read guide, designed to make getting dressed easy. Now and later, when you have a question about appropriate dress, take out this book and use it as your guide.

This book would not have been possible without the close association of my friends at the Airman and Family Readiness Center at Offutt Air Force Base, Nebraska, who are on the TAP (Transition Assistance Program) team. My special thanks go to Ernie, Judy, Billie, Dave, Barry, Kevin, Mike, George and Julia. I also want to acknowledge and thank Bill Christensen from Nebraska Workforce Development. I especially thank my audiences from the United States military for their feedback and input; this is the inspiration for writing the book. I want to thank the audiences from various universities, the business community and organizations for their feedback and support.

This book is frank, direct and to the point. Its purpose is to help you help yourself. Whatever the situation, you will know how to dress appropriately and consistently and display a positive image. My message is this: Image defines you. Clothing is your signature. So let's start getting dressed.

* Please notice quotes and comments highlighted at the beginning of each chapter. These comments are from letters and e-mails received by Bel Air Fashions from participants in Dick Lerner's workshops.

Wardrobe Planner

I've even written a chapter to help you plan your purchases. These lists give you suggestions for things you might want to add to your wardrobe now and over time. You'll find good advice for any stage in your career, no matter where life leads you. Rome wasn't built in a day, and a good wardrobe can't be built overnight either. Use this book to help you *Dress Like the Big Fish* without having to worry if you have made the right decisions. Have fun!

As you might guess, putting illustrations into this book would date it rather quickly. Today's "Power Tie" might change to something else in a year, the lapel of the best suit model may increase in two. In the interest of providing you with the most up-to-date information possible, we will update our website with illustrations and specific styles and colors available at any given time.

Visit us at www.DressLikeTheBigFish.com today.

1

Your Image Defines You

The importance of dress and appearance cannot be overstated. They tell the person you are meeting that they are important to you. You only have one chance to make a first impression...feeling confident that you have the right wardrobe allows you to focus in on the content of that meeting instead of wondering if you look the part.
– Best Regards, Beth Olson (*See Introduction)

How many times a week do you ask yourself or others "What do I wear?" It can be confusing and stressful. Wearing the right thing can get you where you want to be; wearing the wrong thing can be detrimental to your career and your lifestyle. This book has been set up for easy use no matter what situation you have to get dressed for. You'll find answers to the most difficult "What do I wear?" questions from the interview, business meetings, casual events, even weddings. If you have to get dressed and you want to succeed in any setting, you'll find it here.

Like so many people, you want to know how to package yourself, blending your dress and image together. You can dress to enhance your image. Clothing helps differentiate you from everyone else – it's your signature.

Before business casual or casual dress in the workplace came along, the standard of dress was a professional suit, white shirt and a tie for a man and a skirted suit, a white shirt or blouse and scarf for a woman.

From traditional to casual, the changing dress code

In the robust economy of the mid and late 1990s – when there were more jobs than people – dress codes were relaxed. From the start of this century, the economy has been coming off its highs and reaching new lows – and in contrast to the dress codes, the economic atmosphere is not relaxed. Companies that didn't react in time are gone.

In the 1990s, casual dress was used as a draw to get and keep employees. A relaxed dress code was thought of as a benefit. There was no cost to the company – or was there?

Professional (traditional)/ Business casual/Casual

In full employment and when business was bountiful, companies relaxed policies. Among items relaxed was the dress code. The more relaxed the dress became, so did the time at work. It was not uncommon for the workweek to last from 4.5 to 5 days. When Friday noon came, employees would take off.

Dress for many companies Monday through Friday or Tuesday through Thursday was formal or business casual or a combination of both. But on Friday, casual sometimes turned into sloppy casual. For some companies the casual attitude carried over to Monday mornings. The productive workweek now was Tuesday, Wednesday and Thursday. Casual dress led to casual attitudes, sloppiness and loss of productivity.

Studies have shown the correlation of employees dressed in more formal attire; they are more productive and pay more attention to detail. It was also shown that employees take advantage of the workplace more when allowed to dress in casual wear with no defined dress code. People wore to work what they would wear to cut their yard, or to the gym, or even their weekend running around clothes – old tattered clothes and jeans with holes in them. The workplace was as sloppy as the dress.

Many companies regretted the decision to implement casual dress without a full written dress code. They wrestled with the issue of casual dress. Like a hot potato, they didn't know what to do with it. Not creating a well-defined and consistent dress code proved to be counterproductive. The choice was to keep casual dress in the workplace or yank the program and go back to traditional dress. For many companies this was not the answer.

Casual wear in the office came about in the late 1980s when technology firms in the Silicon Valley deemed it not necessary for backroom employees to dress in a jacket, shirt and tie. Most of these employees didn't have direct client contact. So a relaxed dress code was born. By the mid 1990s, casual wear in the office was at its apex as thousands of companies each week were making the change over from formal dress to casual dress in the workplace.

Today there is a shift away from sloppy casual dress in the workplace. As the economy has contracted, business conditions have become very challenging. Companies are fighting for survival. Steps are being taken to insure their ability to do business, maintain market share and, most importantly, meet the expectations of their clients. In a down economy, losing customers to the competition is not an option.

For some firms, formal dress is not required all the time. Business casual has evolved – it is a bridge between formal and casual. Business casual works most of the time, if not all the time. The fabrics have a dressier appearance – a top and bottom will complete an outfit or coordinate back to a jacket. Mixing and matching is the key because the wardrobe can be dressed up, dressed down and dressed right.

Business casual dress should have the same look as a suit – even when a suit is not required. If you know your daily and weekly calendar, you can plan for first-time client meetings, unexpected meetings or unannounced clients. While a shirt, blouse, shell, knit top, slacks or skirt might be all that is required in the office, keep a jacket in your office, so if something comes up on a moment's notice, you will be ready to go.

The interview wardrobe

Where to start? Let's define a good plan – one that gets results and pays dividends. This includes planning your wardrobe so you can adapt to any situation that comes up during the interview process and also allows you to transition to your new job. You don't want one wardrobe for interviewing and another for work. You have to be able to mix-and-match your wardrobe, to dress it up or down, and to dress well.

Give yourself plenty of time to plan out your interview wardrobe; in fact, before you send out your resume, have your interview wardrobe ready to go. A careful and well-configured wardrobe will pay for itself many times over. Don't be in a rush – allow yourself several weeks or even months to find, purchase and assemble your wardrobe.

A wardrobe with no planning becomes very expensive. For example, you may not have the right pieces or enough clothes to get you through interviewing. If all you have is formal clothing and the models, colors and fabrics don't allow you to mix-and-match, the apparel you have assembled may be good only for interviewing. The interview wardrobe becomes quite expensive if some or all the companies tell you follow-up interviews may be business casual or casual. Once you get the job, the dress code may be a combination of professional, business casual or casual.

Many firms still require interview candidates to dress in a suit. This is an employer's market; there are more people than jobs, and companies are being extremely selective. Who they hire is based on the individual's knowledge, skills, image, how they are unique, how they will fit in and what they will bring to the job. When it comes down to the final hiring (with knowledge and skills being comparable), image is often the deciding factor.

Know what companies require for interview dress. Ask. If you are told formal, business casual or casual, you will know how to assemble your apparel. Planning a wardrobe takes time. Not only does it have to carry you through the interview process, your clothing has to transition you to your job.

First and second interviews establish your knowledge and skills; third, fourth and subsequent interviews leading to the final hiring defines your ability to dress from a suit to casual. It helps the company see if you match what they are looking for. If you don't think your dress and appearance will make a difference, think again.

As a final hiring decision is near, keep yourself in the hunt. You cannot control the elements or the environment around you, but you can control how you dress and the image you project. This process defines you and makes the strongest possible statement about yourself. The key is to differentiate yourself so you are remembered for who you are, your uniqueness and what you will bring to the job.

TIP

Dress for one to two levels above the job you are seeking. Dress the best you can in what you can afford, because now it is your time to shine.

When interviewing, dress to get the job, not to make a fashion statement. You don't want to hear, "You are not what we are looking for." Instead, you want to send out the strongest possible message to the company – "I am the person you are looking for!" with their response being, "You are exactly what we are looking for!"

Avoid common mistakes that undermine your dress and image. People often put their education, skill and ability above their dress and image – but these could be the important assets that you alone own. For many companies image is very important because employers seek out individuals who fit into company culture. Those who will not dress appropriately for the interview get sorted out and passed over.

Maintaining your successful image

Once you get the job, it is important to keep up your dress and image for working with clients, unexpected meetings, business conventions or working with associates. It is especially important if you plan to climb further up the career ladder.

Whether you are interviewing or already are employed, the following points are important steps in maintaining a successful image and wardrobe:

Clothing fit – When selecting your outfit, make sure the articles of clothing you choose fit properly. Apparel that is snug or oversized will undercut your professional image and appearance. For example, a coat that you bought five years ago may have fit you then, but perhaps not now. Our bodies change; nothing looks worse than when something doesn't fit. It looks as if you do not know what you are doing or have just come to terms with how you look. It is no different than putting on dad's or grandpa's suit from ten years ago that happens to be two sizes too big or small for you. Make sure whatever you are wearing makes you look balanced and symmetrical. It's part of the fine-tuning process – it's further proof that you care about the details.

Outdated, old or tattered clothes – Clothing styles change frequently. If you show up in an olive tweed jacket with a wide lapel, tapered body, narrow chest and shoulder, paired up with a burgundy shirt and bell bottom jeans – and look as if you were stuffed into all of it, you will have trouble getting people to take you seriously. Of course, this is an extreme example, but get the point? The emphasis will be directed toward your clothing and not on you. Clothing should never enter the room before you do. Successful dress eliminates body distractions and keeps the focus of your image on your face and eyes.

Out-of-date clothing puts you in a time capsule. Fabrics, colors and models all change. The cycle of what's current in apparel trends averages three to five years. Be proactive about your wardrobe. It's important to dress in current styles that emphasize your image and helps you present an entire package that puts forth your knowledge and skills effectively.

The most important point is to look your best, whether you're dressed up or dressed down, whatever your size or personality. Being poised and certain is how you wish to be seen, and this image will carry you a long way.

2

The Power of Image

*ick Lerner's expertise on professional dress
and appearance not only educated me on
the importance of adhering to the professional
standard employers expect of employees, but
also showed me how to achieve it. His contribution
to the TAPS program enabled me to keep the
professional appearance I had in the military and
transition it into the professional civilian arena.*

– Respectfully, Tyler Paige

Power of image is the packaging and delivery of your knowledge and skills. You can make a potent statement about yourself by creating an outer package with your choice of clothing and appearance.

Image is your most important asset because you have total control. Your image needs to be positive and energized, as well as credible, consistent and reliable. Don't let a negative image create a barrier around you.

Studies have been done over the years on image. Albert Mehrabian, Professor Emeritus at UCLA, has formulated his 7/38/55 guideline:

- 7% of your image is what you say
- 38% is how you say it and
- 55% is who and what you are

Your image is your chief attribute in terms of communication, visibility and credibility. It makes you unique and memorable. In the interview process, your image is what you leave behind and how you differentiate yourself from other job candidates. It is often why you get or do not get gainfully employed over somebody else. As I stated before, when knowledge and skills are equal, then your image is a powerful tool that says, "I am the most qualified."

Image is not just for the job interview or work, but for day-to-day activities. It is meeting the expectations of our peers, clients, family and others. Image is defined by verbal (what you say and how you say it) and nonverbal (how you present yourself, your gestures, your facial expressions). You can't really put ability above image – they go hand-in-hand in the minds of people you meet. Your job is to make sure they correlate to each other and support one another; your abilities and skills are enhanced by your image and your image is a spotlight for your skills and abilities.

When communicating, it is imperative to maintain strong eye contact and eliminate any distractions below the neck. In other words, an inappropriately flashy tie would be distracting when you communicate with someone else, just as a sloppy pair of shorts might interfere with a professional message you are delivering.

Another research study outlined the 90/10 rule:

90% of your communication is verbal (with concentration on your eyes and hearing your message from your mouth)

10% or less of communication is nonverbal (what you wear, your body language, which is why you will not want to cause distractions that take away from your verbal communication)

You will either make or break how your message is heard through all the noise and clutter in today's business environment. The key is to keep the audience focused on you and eliminate all distractions so you come across effectively. If the focus is below your neck, your message may be for naught.

TIP

You never want your clothing to go into the room before you as a distraction, or to become the center of attention.

Loud colors, wrinkled fabrics, misfit garments, dated or worn clothing, or inappropriate styles can cause distractions. Powerful dress, in other words, is that of silence; you make no "noise" when properly dressed. Clothing that works does not draw attention, but defines the look you want to project and reinforces the image you wish to deliver.

3

No Second Chances to Make a Great First Impression

ick Lerner has quite literally transformed my attire from olive drab to distinguished; from functional to fashionable (without losing any comfort); from survival in the field to survival in the boardroom (exuding confidence in appearance and demeanor). His advice was absolutely invaluable in my transition from soldier to private sector executive. To visit with Dick is like meeting a Maharishi on top of a tall Tibetan Mountain to discover the "meaning of life" or at least "the meaning of dressing for success."

– Rob Madden, Colonel, US Army (Ret)

You have 10 to 15 seconds to make a first impression, and you don't get a second chance to make that first impression. Strong and favorable impressions are lasting, and weak first impressions are almost impossible to shake. Those first few seconds are your window of opportunity to make a positive and lasting impression. So if you are going to sell yourself, this is the time you want to bring out the best in you. Be prepared.

You want to come into an interview situation for the first time and set yourself apart from other candidates. You want to present an entire package, including dress, image and appearance, that says "I am the one you seek." It shows you "sweated all the details." You have taken the time assembling a wardrobe that "fits," and your "grooming" details pull everything together.

In contrast, someone who thinks his or her "ability" is more important than their "image" would not plan a wardrobe accordingly. That individual may show up in clothing that is ill fitting, disheveled, and may look as if he or she just "rolled out of bed." This image sends the message, "I don't sweat the small details." It basically shows sloppy attitude, sloppy work – a prospective employee who may not be very productive. This leads the company to say simply, "You are not what we are looking for." This individual gets passed over for someone who fits the company better.

Who would you hire or want to do business with? You cannot control the environment around you or things that happen. However you can control you. What does this mean? A great first impression does not just happen. It takes planning and practice. Planning takes careful consideration – how you want to be taken – how you want to be seen.

Your impression is composed of everything about you from the time you took your first breath and everything along the way that got you to this point. Image is something you develop. You are not born with it.

Components that make up your image are your education, life experiences, your personality (vulnerable, regular or overbearing – see chapter 5 for more on this), communication skills (how do you use language, both verbal and nonverbal, voice inflection, hand, body and head gestures and eye movements and eye contact; are you viewed as humorous, serious or combination; are you approachable or not), social manners, business etiquette, and whether you are viewed as credible, reliable and consistent.

Image is a work in motion; it is not something that happens overnight. It has to be nurtured and refined how you want to be seen. It takes practice, practice and more practice.

Image is head-to-toe. What you see is what everyone else sees. Get in front of family, friends and peers and have them critique you. Take criticism constructively and work to improve it. Practice working on your image and the impression you make so you become comfortable with the process. Stand in front of a three-way mirror to see yourself from the front, side and back. Have a checklist. Make sure your clothing fits properly, is pressed, current and in good shape. Make sure there is nothing about your non-clothing items to cause distractions that could take away from your image.

The end result is to keep the audience focused on your face, not on your body or your clothing. It's maintaining eye contact so your message is heard, and presenting yourself in a way that insures that your message is remembered.

Now you are ready to market yourself. Whether interviewing or working with clients, you have defined yourself to be effective in any situation. The emphasis is on you and your abilities — and your image underscores your credibility.

Image checklist for non-clothing items

- ☐ **Hair:** Is it clean? Is there dandruff or flaking? Hair brushed? Good cut? No bushy neck? For men, a haircut should be short and conservative. For women, the cut should be above the shoulders. For important interviews and for meetings, hair should be pulled back and up, and secured with a conservative hair clip. Does it look good with the shape of your face and glasses? Are there straggly hairs? Does your hair look natural? Oily or too dry?

- ☐ **Eyeglasses:** Are frames current? Do they have color? (Monochromatic blends give no contrast. Frames with color lead the audience right to your eyes, which are the focal point of your communication. Are your lenses clean, clear and not scratched? (Lenses cannot change color coming in from the outdoors to inside. Your audience has to be able to see your eyes. Your eyes cannot be covered by smoke-colored lenses.) Do your eyeglasses complement the shape of your face, eyes and hairstyle? (You cannot have distractions occurring or fighting each other. Everything between your eyes, glasses and hairstyle has to be in harmony and complement each other. Nothing can get in the way to take away from your message. Your eyes are the focal point of your communication so your message is heard.)

☐ **Cosmetics**: If you are covering blemishes, does the color blend with your skin tone? Does it make you look pale or washed out? Do you have an appropriate amount of makeup on for the workday? (Cosmetics are used to lightly cover and highlight the face.) Mascara applied lightly (if used)? Did you apply lipstick lightly and not draw attention?

☐ **Facial hair:** Is your beard, mustache or goatee trimmed, neat and not straggly? Is the color the same as your hair? Does it complement your hairstyle? No hair coming out of the nostrils or earlobes? No whiskers above the lips, side-of-the-mouth, face, neck or under earlobes? (Facial hair is also a concern for women as well and should be removed.)

☐ **Fingernails:** Are your nails trimmed, clean and manicured? (Make sure your fingernails don't look nail bitten. No dirt under the nails.) Do your nails look healthy? Fingernail polish should not draw attention or try to make a fashion statement with the color or length of nails or adornments on the nails.

Clothing

Make sure whatever you are wearing is current, in good shape, clean and pressed and properly fit. The jacket needs to fit around your neck, back of neck, chest, waist, hips and seat with no excess fabric, bulges or puckers. A jacket is your major wardrobe piece. You do not want it to become a visual obstacle that could detract from your overall message and image.

Jacket/shirts/blouses – If you are not wearing a jacket, make sure your blouse, shirt, shell or knit top is properly fit and balanced to your body, front and back. Make sure it is tucked in neatly. Make sure the fabric is in good shape, not stained, tattered or frayed. Whatever you have on, make sure it is pressed well. It is important to pay particular attention how your top makes you look. Remember, a jacket hides many of the body's unique fit features, so when not wearing a jacket, be sure your top looks good on its own and fits right.

Slacks/skirts – Make sure the bottoms you wear have a good appearance, are well pressed, properly fit, not tattered or old. Check that the length is not too short or too long, and you look balanced and symmetrical.

Socks/hosiery – Make sure there are no holes in your socks or hosiery, that they are not discolored, tattered or old. Nothing you wear should bunch or sag, including your socks.

Shoes – Shoes should be in good shape and the color should complement the outfit. Shoes are one of the most important articles you wear. They can be high maintenance. Make sure they have a good shine, don't look worn or out of date. The worst mistake made is wearing shoes that look like they should have been thrown away a long time ago.

Accessories – Accessories should not be noticed. Don't wear too much. You don't want to detract from your message. Accessories should not make "noise" or be gaudy. For more on accessories, see chapter 15.

You are creating a marketing package – not a fashion package. You don't want anything to get in the way of your message. Your clothing and non-clothing items should be in harmony with one another.

4

From Suits to Jeans
and Back Again

think the scariest thing to me is that I truly didn't know I wasn't dressing right. All I knew was that I was getting passed over for promotions and assignments that had high visibility. I met Dick Lerner at an event and everything changed. He taught me the things he put in this book and my life immediately changed because I commanded more presence.

– Sincerely, Candace W.

Before casual dress appeared in the workplace, companies expected employees to dress professionally. Suits were the norm and worn to work daily. Blazers or sports coats, slacks, shirts and ties were alternatives for men; women wore skirted suits or blazers, pattern jackets and skirts, blouses, scarves or even bows. Pant suits were hardly ever acceptable in a professional setting. This was the standard of dress for American business. Some firms never got away from it.

"What goes around...comes around." Many companies experimented with one form or another of casual dress. Relaxing dress codes in the early and mid 1990s was an attraction to get new employees and keep the ones they had. This was viewed as a company benefit to employees with little cost to the company… or was there?

In the early 1990s the new economy was emerging, new companies, industries were up and coming. Anything connected with computers was part of the economic boom and its derivatives. There were more jobs than people. Companies saw a relaxed dress code as part of the norm.

Jackets and ties for these new industries became a thing of the past. For most firms a skeleton dress code existed – each company was different. In most cases tank tops, cut offs and sandals were not allowed, but almost everything else was permitted. Eventually dress became a haunting issue for many companies because of lack of communication, lack of rules and a misunderstanding of the terminology on almost everyone's part.

When meeting a new client for the first time, the question was posed, "What is your company dress?" In the established or old economy, this question was never asked, because first-time meetings with new clients required professional dress. Luckily, for many companies, this is still the case.

Dress codes that were not clearly defined caused significant problems. Employee dress could be what one would wear to wash the car, work out in at the gym, cut the yard, walk the dog and other informal events. It became a fiasco and a nightmare. For many employees, a non-dress code became a license to wear anything: "Give someone an inch, they will take a mile."

Clothes worn to work in many cases were misfit, old, tattered and stained, not pressed and had a messy appearance. During the early 1990s up to the market downturn of early 2000, dress and appearance became an issue companies had to address as the economy slipped.

Dress and attention to detail became sloppy and had its effect on attitudes toward work and productivity. Along with casual clothes came a casual attitude and sloppiness.

In 2000, the new economy all but collapsed with the recession. The dot.coms vanished. Technology companies struggled. In a short two and a half years, the economy did a 180-degree about face – a paradigm shift. The severity is more than the last several recessions, and its effect is lingering longer than anyone expected. The result is more people are looking for work than there are jobs. The hiring environment is very selective.

Companies began searching, redefining and repackaging themselves for their economic survival. Struggling firms couldn't perform customer service and in many cases lost long-term customers. They could no longer meet their growing expectations. Firms had to evaluate where they were and where they were going. With the tight economy and huge unemployment, it became an employers' market.

September 11, 2001, was an event unlike any other our economy has gone through. It accelerated many processes that eventually would have come to the surface. Since that date many firms have blended many of the new economy attributes back to the old economy. Among those changes is the dressing up of casual wear.

Many firms abandoned casual dress. This form of dress didn't work for the workplace and something had to be done. Trends and cycles come and go. The intent of casual wear in the workplace seemed to be a good concept at the time. It was viewed as an employee benefit with little cost to the company, but the cost was far greater than anticipated. If more attention had been given to defining standard dress codes and consistent implementation, casual dress could have been successful.

The dressing up of casual will be adapted to each firm's needs. A suit and tie may not be required, nor will a pair of khakis and a polo. These are the issues being defined at this writing – defining dress that is acceptable.

5

Know Yourself

I first walked into Bel Air Fashions around 20 years ago with a friend who was looking for a sport coat. I left the store that day with 4 coats of my own and that was the beginning of a relationship that still continues to this day. Their fashion sense, service and helpfulness is second to none. They taught me how to buy off the rack, as well as how to order a custom-made suit that will fit perfectly and look spectacular. Their knowledge of what's right in the business world is extremely useful. They should be a must-see prior to job interviews or any type of meeting where you have to impress others. If only their clothes didn't last so long, I'd have an excuse to go back and get more stuff.

– Dennis DeRoin, MD, Family Physician

Know yourself. That's the foundation for your professional and business casual dress and the image you wish to have.

Give yourself plenty of time and develop a plan that leads to successful employment of choice. Never be in a hurry to assemble your wardrobe. Before you even think about your interview clothing, first define the jobs that you are interested in.

Once you have assembled a list, among your questions for the company should include interview dress. For each firm you are pursuing, find out if the dress requirement is professional, business casual or casual. You need to know this information so you can assemble your interview wardrobe. You need your clothing to take you from the interview to your new job. If not planned properly and thought out, your wardrobe can become quite expensive. You don't want to have one wardrobe for interviewing and another for work.

Before you make your first clothing purchase, you need to know your body type and personality. Body types are small, regular and large frame. Personality types are vulnerable, regular and overbearing. Personality reflects directly on body type, image and appearance.

Body type

Large frame: Dress for comfort. Select fabrics that drape and do not cling. It is important to make sure you are balanced and symmetrical in your clothing. Whether you are dressed professionally, business casual or casual, you never want to draw attention to your body.

Select colors that do not draw attention. Fabrics can be solids or small nondescript patterns. These are excellent choices. Texture of fabric is important in determining how it will drape and fit. You never want to look overbearing or intimidating. Large people think they can't look good in their clothes. That isn't so. Preparation, planning and taking your time acquiring your wardrobe is paramount in achieving desired consistent results.

Reflect on your prior wardrobe. What components did you like and dislike in terms of fabric, fit, colors and so forth. Don't repeat past mistakes. Make sure whatever you add to your wardrobe has a purpose, will work with other items in your closet and more importantly gives you the desired look and fit.

You don't have to spend a fortune. Buy for quality and value and get items that will give you multiple uses. Your wardrobe shouldn't be how many clothes you have but the right clothing. A wardrobe that is concise and gives you the ability of dressing it up and down and the ability to mix-and-match on a year round basis is a wardrobe you will be able to plan your daily and weekly calendar around – successfully.

Being large frame is no different than being a regular or small framed individual – you still need to educate yourself what a good fit is when you dress professionally, business casual or casual. Fit your clothing meticulously and consistently – this will pay off many times over. Being large is not a penalty; it's taking care of business and that is paying attention to the small details. It's all the little things you do right that make a difference.

Understand fabric and clothing models. Know what fabrics work with your body type and avoid fabrics that lead to bad fit and appearance. For example, you might select a single-breasted 2 or 3 button suit or a sport jacket, and a flat front or pleated slack. Select models that flow with your body and make you look balanced and symmetrical – not something that fits snugly. Models either complement or detract from your fit. Know which models are right for you and stay away from the ones that aren't. Select colors that make you look friendly and approachable – not overbearing.

Regular frame: Dress for power and authority or friendly and approachable. Your frame size is not intimidating. Never be lax with your appearance. You need to understand what works for your frame when it comes to fabric, models and fit.

Select fabrics that make you look symmetrical, do not cling to your body, and that drape properly. You need to make sure the fit is balanced – not untidy. Fit of clothing needs to be meticulous, so educate yourself what models are best for you, and know what a good fit is. Pay attention to the small details, it makes a big difference in your fit and appearance.

If you are tall and lanky, buy clothing that fills you out, not up and down. Regular size frames are an adaptive fit, so know what is right for you.

Small frame: Similar to large frame people, small frame people may have a problem commanding respect and authority. So select fabrics, models and colors that fill you in appropriately. Colors should be darker to command power and authority. Solid color fabrics are good, and small patterns or nondescript weaves add depth to your appearance. Fit needs to be meticulous and clothing should have a more expensive appearance. It is very important to be consistent in your dress and appearance.

Take note of your past wardrobe to items that gave you problems, and stay away from similar clothing. Select items that are one to two levels higher than you would normally dress. For example, if you are interviewing for a job or a promotion, the clothing you select should be what a manager would wear instead of entry level. It is better to be overdressed than under dressed.

Dress and image, when done right, is an asset, not a liability. If you want to advance in your career, your dress and image show you are ready for anything that comes up. Whether interviewing, conducting business or negotiating, your dress and image shouldn't erode confidence, it should enhance it. This is why you always want to dress to a higher level.

Skin tone

Whether you are large, regular or small frame, know your skin tone type. Skin tone is either warm or cool.

To determine your skin tone, look in the mirror to see if your skin tone has a red or yellow tint. Knowing your skin tone type helps you from washing out or looking sallow in your clothing. If you are red based, you don't want to come off as intimidating. Knowing your skin tone type helps you to determine how certain colors look on you. To get good contrast from the colors you wear, you want to look energized not anemic.

Warm tone: Someone with a warm tone to their skin has a tendency to wash out or look anemic or pale. Skin tone is very fair and may look like it is almost yellow based. Clothing colors that wash you out are light gray, yellow, or tan (orange base). If your skin tone is warm, stay away from these colors. However, tan that is red based has good contrast.

Cool tone: People that have a large frame with a cool skin tone may appear rough and overbearing, especially if their facial features are not smooth. If your skin has a cool tone, stay away from dark colors such as stark navy and black. Color choice should not be a stark contrast, so soften your color choices. In other words use a charcoal blue or gray instead of navy or black to make your appearance softer, not overbearing or intimidating. It makes you look more friendly and approachable. Colors that soften the look are taupe, medium gray, charcoal or slate blue, loden and olive (brown or black tone).

Personality

Know your personality type. You never want this to be a barrier. There are three distinct personality types.

Overbearing: These people can be perceived as intimidating. This quality is often associated with large frame people. Someone who is large and dresses for power and authority and comes off as overbearing and intimidating may not get the message heard. Do not project a stark and harsh image. Dress it down to work in your favor, not against you. Make yourself friendly and approachable so you get your message across.

Regular: Regular personality is adaptive, friendly and approachable. This personality type will dress up for power and authority or dress down to be friendly and approachable. This personality type is not perceived as intimidating or overbearing, nor are they looked at as weak or not able to command authority.

Vulnerable: Often perceived as weak and unable to command authority. Respect is a big issue. Small frame people with slight build are often associated with this personality type. Overcome this by investing in clothing that looks expensive and dark. Dress for power and authority. Once you come across in this manner, your message will be heard. Clothing needs to fill you out. The emphasis needs to be taken off your body and the attention should be drawn to your face and eyes so your message is heard.

Understanding body size and personality type gives you an edge overcoming barriers – not taking away from your message or image.

Interview dress is not simply getting dressed, going to an interview and getting a job. One could only wish it would be this easy. Interview dress is all about you and how you package your image, knowledge and skills. It is how you best use your verbal and non-verbal skills. It is how you bring your image and ability together as one.

Professional dress is about fabric, construction, models, fit and durability. The same is true for business casual and casual. A wardrobe carefully planned will pay off in your success.

6

It's All About the Fabric

It's true. Thank you for teaching me about the importance of good fabrics. I now know what to buy and how long I should expect to keep it! It's already helped me choose a suit that I love!
— A Fan, Bridget Wayson

Fabric is the foundation of your professional, business casual and casual wardrobe. It's all about the fabric. Bad fabric detracts from dress and image because it won't fit, it doesn't wear well and it doesn't last. Knowing about fabric before you start building your wardrobe will enable you to purchase pieces that mix-and-match well and will last.

Nobody is going to grab you and search your clothing to find a label. Buying clothing in this manner is not the way to build a wardrobe – garments accumulated without a plan are a waste of money and are often left hanging in the back of the closet collecting dust. The end result? Nothing goes together and you have wasted a tremendous amount of money.

The purpose of this book is to emphasize how important your image is. If your clothing, especially the fabric, is causing major obstacles for you, then you will not be taken seriously. You never want wrinkled or ill-fitting clothing to be a hindrance in your communication or diminish your appearance.

The quality of fabric is critical in your working wardrobe because all of the fabrics you choose should work together for your various dressing needs. Know the various types of natural and manmade fabrics. This chapter will explain them in detail.

Natural fibers

Wool – Used for jackets, skirts, pants and outerwear

Wool is the fabric of choice. It is a long-wearing natural fiber and has a very professional appearance. Wool often gets a bad rap because it scratches, itches or doesn't hold its shape. That is dependent on the wool selected. There are many different grades.

Among the world's best wool is Merino. The lightest and most delicate fiber is called Pashmina. This is an ultra luxury form of mohair (It comes from a special breed of Himalayan goat and is very expensive – not practical for daily use. I mention it here so you know of its existence). It is Merino wool that allows you to build a magnificent longevity wardrobe. This particular wool is preferred for its strength, smooth silky texture, ability to maintain shape and, most important, longevity.

Merino wool is used for high-quality clothing. When it comes time to shear the sheep, the preferred wool is what comes from the inside – the chest side of the sheep – from the neck to the inside fleece of the stomach and legs. This is soft and rich in lanolin or body oil. Lanolin is considered to be the outstanding attribute in grading quality of wool after it is shorn. This is what keeps the sheep warm and happy. It will feel great to you too!

The grading process occurs at the time the animal is sheared. The droppings on the ground are graded by hand. The more "silk or wet" like to the hand, the higher the quality. Typically the best wool used for fabrics ranges from 90s to 150s in quality. Wool is measured in microns (the width of the wool fibers) and how many threads per square inch (the width of the ply). Example: Super 100s = 100 threads per square inch, Super 120s = 120 threads per square inch. Better wools are 2-ply weave.

The wool on the sheep's back is what keeps it protected from the elements. This is much coarser and dryer. These trimmings are used to make flannel, donegal, tweed and shetland fabrics. Understand the difference between what keeps the animal warm and the wool that protects the animal. It's the wool that keeps the sheep warm that is the preferred choice in fine fabrics.

You'll see these terms: high twist or striated, bengaline, gabardine, faille, twill, covert twill, serge, tricotine, sharkskin, birdseye, pic-n-pic and worsteds. These are some of the many fine fabrics woven of wool. These are the preferred natural fabrics for jackets, skirts and slacks.

Wool densely woven in a two-ply weave is very strong and holds its shape, resists wrinkling and breaking down. It breathes, is ideal for year-round wear, and is one of the most adaptive fabrics. Wool keeps you cool in the summer and warm in the winter, and it does not matter if the climate is dry or damp.

Wool's characteristics and overall appearance may be affected in extreme heat and humidity where it might wrinkle. Normally overnight a high-quality weave will hang and dry out, and the wrinkles will dissipate.

Another term you will often see is "2-ply." This is the wrapping of the vertical and horizontal threads twice (warp and fill) as the yarns are woven and is what gives the thread tensile strength – to resist wrinkling.

When threads aren't wrapped, fabrics are limp and porous and break down prematurely.

It is best to buy only two-ply wool fabrics, since the body is not kind to fabric. We put our clothes through the paces and punish them in a normal day-to-day wearing. If the fabric is not made well, it will wear out too soon.

A densely woven fabric is essential to insure you have a good dependable fabric. If the fabric feels light, wrinkles easily and seems to be transparent, chances are it is a one-ply fabric – avoid these because they can wrinkle and wear out.

The following is a good guide to use when selecting a wool suit, sport coat, pant or skirt (but ask permission from the store before you make the following examination):

The fabric you test should have a "wet" or "silk" like feeling. Your hand should glide across the fabric smoothly, unrestricted and the fabric should not feel coarse. The garment ticket will only say 100% wool, but it will not tell you everything you need to know. If the fabric feels dry, uneven and pricks your skin, chances are you have one-ply low-grade wool. The fabric will not hold its shape, may wrinkle and is not a good fabric to add to your wardrobe.

Squeeze the fabric and release. If it bounces back to its original shape, chances are you have a two-ply fabric. If it doesn't bounce back, it's likely a one-ply fabric.

Tie the fabric in a tight knot, then untie it, the fabric should spring back. If not, then you know this fabric is probably a one-ply fabric and will not be a good choice.

Put your hand inside the fabric. If you can see through the fabric or you see your hand, it means the fabric is porous, does not have good strength, will break down prematurely and the fabric will probably wrinkle. If you see the fabric is densely woven with little see through, then you have chosen a good fabric. Another test is to hold the fabric up to the light. Make sure you cannot see through it like clear wrap. If the fabric looks loosely woven and is not a dense pattern, it will be a problem. Problems that occur include not holding the shape of the garment, fabric will ball or peel, and may tear easily.

Selecting fabrics in this manner is the most important step in knowing how to put a wardrobe together. Finding a high-quality wool fabric will ensure that you have pieces that will look great all day, will last and will provide good opportunities for mixing and matching.

In the care of wool use a handheld or floor model steamer because steam revives the wool and keeps it pressed. A few seconds of steam is all it takes. For finformation on fabric care, see chapter 18.

Today's wool has been improved through technology. Wool fabrics today include stretch, Teflon coating or wrinkle resistance, and many are washable. Pack-n-go wool garments are a result of the breakthrough technologies adapted in the manufacture of wool and other textiles.

Men's and women's suits are now available in travel garments. Women's separates made of stretch wool have been available as a hard finish wrinkle-resistant garment for years. The fabric used is pack-n-go, which means you take it out of your suitcase and it is ready to wear. Wool has come a long way.

Wool is a lifestyle fabric – it adapts to a hectic daily schedule that can be very tough on a fabric, yet wool breathes. The higher quality fabrics like this always look fresh and have great appearance.

The right quality and weight can be worn all year in all climates. The best weight for year-round is approximately 9 to 10 ounces – not too heavy or too light. Fabric goes by weight and stitches-per-inch. You want the wool you select to have the best quality and value for you; it will pay for itself many times over.

Cotton: Used for dress and casual shirts, blouses, polos, slacks and shorts

The ad campaign for cotton calls it "the fabric of your life." It is a natural fiber that breathes and feels comfortable against the skin. Pima and Egyptian are the most preferred, as both of these fibers have a soft "silk" or "wet" like feel, very strong and long lived.

Cotton fabrics that have good value and quality will use Pima and Egyptian cotton in a variety of better dress and casual shirts, blouses, polos, pants, skirts, jackets, suits and outerwear. The fabrics have a smooth silky feel, are a two-ply (horizontal and vertical threads wrapped two times) and are densely woven.

New technologies have been incorporated in the production of cotton fabrics and are described here.

Men's and women's non-iron cotton shirts and blouses are now available. The most popular weave is the 80s two-ply 100 percent cotton pinpoint. The fabric manufacturer chemically bakes the non-iron process in. It is a breakthrough technology.

These non-iron shirts and blouses are made to never require ironing. Wash at home with two or three other shirts of the same color in a cold water wash, permanent press cycle and mild detergent. Then, put in the dryer, use permanent press and delicate, after about 15 to 20 minutes, take out and hang up. These garments are ready to wear.

If you forget to take them out of the dryer, and the shirts are wrinkled, it's alright. Get a spray bottle, fill with water and spray shirts lightly, just enough to make them damp. Put back in the dryer for 15 or 20 minutes, then hang up.

These fabrics are easy to care, easy maintenance, and shrinkage is minimal. The big benefit is their fresh appearance.

The significance of non-iron shirt fabrics is they don't look wrinkled at the end of the day. This is a big plus for dress and a professional look. When a fabric breaks down, it makes the wearer look messy, which is not the case with the non-iron fabrics. This is especially important for professional, business casual and casual apparel.

Non-iron cotton men's slacks are also available. This is possible because the non-iron technology is incorporated during the manufacturing of the fabric. This process stays embedded during the life of the garment.

Cotton is a wonderful natural fiber – but the traditional type of cotton does wrinkle. High-quality cotton such as Pima and Egyptian will last and not break down. Enhancing non-iron technology with these quality cotton fibers creates a high performance fabric.

In review, when acquiring cotton fabrics as part of your wardrobe, whether iron or non-iron, remember to buy high-quality cotton – Pima or Egyptian. Cotton fibers have a "silky or wet feel," are densely woven and have a two-ply weave. Cotton that is dry, coarse, loosely woven and stiff should be avoided; it will break down prematurely and you will need to replace more often.

Silk: Used for scarves, ties, dress and casual shirts, blouses, slacks, shorts, sport coats and suits

One of nature's strongest fibers comes from the silk worm. Discovered thousands of years ago and often considered the fabric of royalty, silk is commonly found in men's ties, bow ties, ascots, vests, shirts, sport coats, pants, outerwear and suits. Silk is used in women's scarves, blouses, jackets, slacks, skirts, dresses and outerwear.

Silk by itself will wrinkle in clothing. It is a strong fiber that will last but lacks "fiber strength" so that it does not shed wrinkling. In clothing it is often blended with wool to hold its shape and create a luxurious feel.

Silk is most notably used in neckwear for men and women. If you see "mm" on the label, this is how silk is weighed. Quality silk neckwear often will range from 30 to 40 oz mm. The more it weighs, the better the quality.

Silk neckwear can be made of many different weaves. Among the most popular and best quality is a silk woven. A woven often will have a textured surface; it has a tight weave that will prevent the silk from unraveling.

Some of the other popular weaves are ancient madder, satin and twill.

Tencel: Used for slacks, shorts, shirts, blouses, sport coats and suits

Tencel comes from the wood chip pulp of trees. When compared to a ball of cotton, both tencel and cotton have a similar look and feel. Tencel is denser and weighs more. It is used in shirts, slacks, suit jackets and slacks.

Tencel fabrics are used more for business casual and casual. Tencel by itself has a soft feel, but if not woven with another fabric that resists wrinkling, it will wrinkle. Tencel is often combined with microfiber in the manufacture of slacks and jackets. When woven in a twill weave (twill is a diagonal mini-rope weave – similar to a gabardine weave, but thicker), it has a suede-like cast to the finish of the fabric.

Shirt fabrics can be made of 100 percent tencel, although often blended with silk, cotton or microfiber; tencel drapes and does not cling. When blended with other fibers, it will hold its shape.

Linen: Used for shirts, blouses, slacks, shorts, sport coats and suits

Linen is a "flax fabric." It is very porous or loosely woven. It does not hold its shape, shrinks, sags and bags and should not be used for day-to-day professional, business casual or casual wear and never for an interview. It is best suited for weekend and resort wear. It is lightweight and breathes, but it looks as if you have slept in the fabric shortly after putting the garment on.

For those who wear linen, understand how the fabric will perform and only wear when you needn't be concerned about its appearance.

Manmade fibers

Microfiber: women's separates – jacket, skirt and pants; excellent for men's business casual separates – jackets and slacks

Microfiber is a manmade fabric. On labels, its description will be 100 percent microfiber (polyester), 100 percent polyester, polyester/polynosnic or polyester/viscose. These are the different fiber contents woven in flat finish piece goods, tricotine (woven mini square or linear weave), fishbone (small reverse saw tooth weave), twills (raised diagonal mini rope) and gabardine (cut on a 45-degree diagonal bias is a small tight mini cord) weaves.

Excellent characteristics of microfiber are the following: it has a flat finish (no sheen) and it does not look like a polyester. It has good body and won't go limp. In other words the fabric, when woven, has good density, which allows the fabric to drape not cling.

The microfiber family of fabrics is excellent for business casual and casual slacks. Microfiber is found in women's suit separates – which is excellent for professional and business casual wear. Having a jacket, skirt and pant allows the wearer to dress up and dress down and mix-and-match with different jackets, skirts, slacks, blouses and knit tops.

Microfiber is used more for slacks in menswear. There are some jackets available that match the pants that would be suitable business casual. Microfiber is a good fabric for men's slacks for business casual and casual.

Microfiber slacks can be mixed-and-matched with men's wool blazers, wool and wool and silk sport coats. Good quality microfiber fabrics often can't be distinguished between good woolen slack fabrics.

Microfiber is easy care, pack-n-go and wrinkle-resistant, and many of the polyester versions are washable. Excellent fabric for travel.

Viscose/rayon: Often combined with microfiber on certain fabric weaves such as a gabardine or twill weave – for jackets, skirts or pants. These fibers are good for helping fabric maintain shape.

Nylon: Gives strength to fabric – normally used in small percentage in the make up of a microfiber fabric.

Lycra: Gives fabric the ability to stretch. Normal make up in a fabric can be from 1 to 6 percent. Keeps fabric from wrinkling and helps to maintain shape.

Now that you have a basic understanding of the fabrics, let's start our wardrobe building with clothes for the professional business person.

7

Know Your Leather

*F*abulous education I didn't know I needed.
I didn't realize there were so many things to
consider when choosing leather products. I've
made some mistakes, but with your help, I know
what I need to do. Amazing!
— Theodore Xanan, Consultant

Why is it so important? Outside of your clothing, leather accessories are items that can make or break your outfit.

Leather that is cheaply made looks it and doesn't last as long as it should. Good leather products are expensive. You do not want the cheapest nor the most expensive leather, but those that will last and look like high-quality items for a long time. Their quality emphasizes and complements your overall outfit and image.

There is a difference in leather, how it is processed and finished – smooth, grain or embossed to look like an exotic skin such as alligator.

Coja Leatherline of Canada states, "The best leather is known as full top grain. This premium leather has not been buffed or sanded.

The quality of the finished leather is affected by the finishing process and will be apparent in its softness and suppleness as well as the uniformity and penetration of the colour." (Source: Coja Furniture Manufacturer – experts in fine leather).

When it comes to leather it doesn't matter if it is something you wear or sit on – the principles of fine leather are the same. Top grain leathers are used extensively for the auto and home industry; this chapter will deal with the best leathers to look for when buying coats, jackets, belts, braces, shoes, wallets, purses, folios, wallets or watchbands.

Leather should have a supple hand or rich feel when you touch it. The leather is not stretched or thinned down, and it shouldn't feel stiff. Cheaply made leathers are thin, tend to peel and will likely lose their finish. These types of leathers have a dry feel to the touch and almost look like vinyl.

There are wonderful processing techniques used that can make a leather skin look antiqued, stained or even accentuate the grain of the hide. A good leather skin can last for years. With age, good leather gets softer and is a pleasure to wear.

Kip or calf-skin leathers are ideal for wardrobe building. Good quality leathers like these will last for a long time.

These leathers have a duller finish. The leathers have not been stretched, so they absorb the finish and maintain it longer. Stretched leathers are thinner and don't maintain the finish very well. Today's finishes used in leather dying have higher volumes of silicone, thus the finish has a tendency to rub off on thinner leather.

Here is how to tell the difference: When you have a thin leather, the finish will rub off and tear prematurely. It may crack and wrinkle. A thicker leather holds the finish and will get softer over time; it has a very smooth feel. The leather holds its shape no matter how many times it is worn; it has a quality look.

Below are some of the different leather terms and their meanings.

Kip – hide used from a young calf or lamb; the hide is not mature like an older animal. Leather is thicker and has a supple hand and

dyes penetrate and create a beautiful finish. Very durable and can be refinished in the future after prolonged use.
Ideal for use in leather belts, braces, purses, folios and briefcases.

Calf – hide from a young male or female cow calf. Similar to Kip, has wonderful absorbent properties, takes dyes well, finish doesn't rub off easily, and is not prone to peeling. Depending how the leather is finished, it can have a smooth or grain finish.
Ideal use is for belts, braces, shoes, purses, folios/briefcases, watchbands and wallets; can be used for leather jackets or coats.

Matisse – hide from a special breed of lamb; bred between the lamb and goat family. The hide is drum-dyed. The leather is very supple and soft. Final finish is buffed to fine suede that feels like silk.
Ideal use is for dress gloves.

Glove – hide comes from several animals including lamb, kid, pig and deer. The hide is processed to be very soft and supple.
Its final finish has stretch, which is ideal for use in dress gloves.

Nubuc – is a process where a hide is buffed to create a finish between a smooth leather and suede. It is buffed and brushed (outer skin side) and the finish is very fine and supple.
Ideal use in belts, braces, wallets, purses, folios/briefcases, gloves and shoes.

Suede – is a process where split leather has been buffed to remove the smooth surface. It feels like very soft fur.
Ideal use in shoes, wallets, belts, braces, purses, folios, watchbands, coats and jackets.

Kid – hide from a young goat. It is young leather which has its own natural characteristics. The leather has a soft and supple feel.
Ideal use of kidskin is for dress and casual shoes.

Aniline – is a process used to dye leather. Similar to staining wood, it absorbs all the way through the skin. Aniline leather enhances the natural beauty of the skin. It is supple and thicker, maintains finish very well and is durable – not likely to peel.

Ideal use of aniline leather is for belts, braces, shoes, purses, folios, wallets and watchbands.

Deerskin – hide comes from deer. Leather has a very soft and supple feel. Has a grainy surface; absorbs dyes very well, thicker and durable. This leather maintains its finish very well.
Ideal use of deerskin is for gloves, belts, shoes, wallets and leather jackets.

Lambskin – hide from a lamb. This young hide has a very rich and supple hand. Hide can be smooth or buffed to a grain finish. There are many ways it can be processed and finished. It takes dyes very well. It is high-quality leather.
Ideal use of lambskin is used for wallets, watchbands, folios, briefs cases, coats and jackets.

Plongé – is taking a lambskin leather and drum dyeing it to be very soft and supple finish; it has a lot of body and a grainy surface. The final process is aniline that is dyed through the whole skin and enhances its natural beauty.
Ideal use is in leather jackets and coats, wallets, belts, folios, briefcases or computer briefs.

Shell Cordovan – hide of the horse. (Not to be confused with Cordovan Leather from the Mouflon sheep) Shell Cordovan is a very hard surface. It is an expensive leather and should be worn with care because it is hard to keep a rich finish on this leather.
Ideal use is for shoes, belts, purses, folios and briefcases.

Shearling – hide of sheep. The wool is attached to the hide. The underside of the hide is the outer portion of the coat and the wool is against the body. As mentioned in the book, shearling is lightweight and warm, making it a good choice for a coat or jacket.
Ideal use is for winter jackets and coats. Other ideal use of shearling is for slippers, the lining of dress and business casual shoes, hats and gloves.

Buffalo – It is soft and supple – a thicker leather. Its color is natural and doesn't need to be processed.
Ideal use is for shoes – dress and business casual – belts, wallets, watchbands and jackets.

Elk – Elk is a member of the deer family. It is similar to deer – soft full grain leather that can be left natural or dyed.
Ideal use is for shoes (business casual and casual), belts, wallets and jackets.

Elk and Buffalo were not mentioned elsewhere in this book nor are they widely used, but you should be aware of their existence in case you come across them while shopping. They are thicker leather and are ideal for more casual, outdoor and weekend wear.

Pigskin – Pigskin is natural suede with good body to the hide. Pigskin can be found mainly in gloves, wallets, watchbands, shirts and jackets. It is mentioned in the book for use in gloves.
Ideal for outdoor and weekend wear.

Exotic skins – Used for production of shoes, belts, braces, wallets, purses, folios, briefcases, jackets and coats. Includes hides from alligator, crocodile, ostrich, snake and eel.

These skins are expensive. They are thinner, need to be pampered and cannot withstand mistreatment. If abused they can tear – so they should be used for special occasions.

Leather care

Suede and Nubuc – The best care is to brush. There are special brushes that you can purchase for suede and Nubuc with instructions how to brush in the proper manner.

Sometimes it is suggested to use a soft eraser to gently clean a spot. Do not dry clean unless absolutely necessary! If you have a problem with your Nubuc or suede product, contact a company that specializes in leather and suede cleaning only.

Leather – This includes any smooth or grain leather mentioned – the best care is to wipe with a soft clean cloth. If your leather has dried out, there are special lotions, mink oil and leather balms available.

A special word of caution, do not automatically apply any lotion. Find out at the time of purchase what type of care to give and what can be used on the skin. Not every lotion, balm or mink oil can be used. If you use the wrong product, you can take the finish off your leather or void any warranties that may exist with the product.

If leather gets wet, you need to let it dry out naturally. Do not stand outside in driving rain or snow for extended periods of time because water will ruin the finish.

If your garment gets damaged due to the elements, take it to a specialized leather cleaner as quickly as possible so it can be restored. Take your shoes, belts, purses, folios and briefcases to a good shoe repairer for restoration.

Sources

Coja Leatherline of Canada – www.coja.com
Indian Leather Portal – www.indianleatherportal.com
Siegel of California – www.siegelofca.com

8
Suits Me:
Professional Dress for Men

*If you're looking for straightforward, no-nonsense
advice on how to look classic, stylish and
impressive, pay attention to what Dick Lerner says.*
— Larry Bradley, Publisher

For men, professional dress includes the tailored, matched business suit, dress shirt, tie and dress shoes. For women, professional dress means a tailored matched skirted suit, dress blouse or shell, neutral hose and a closed-toe pump shoe.

Many companies never abandoned professional dress to adopt business casual. Today it is not unusual for companies to have three or four days of professional dress and set Fridays as business casual.

Why is professional dress so important? Companies have a corporate culture to maintain. Their associates are a mirror image of that culture, reflecting their clients' expectations of that company and its staff. A company cannot afford not to meet those expectations.

Companies seek individuals who will fit into their "corporate culture." For those seeking employment, when told the interviews are formal, make sure you are dressed appropriately. If you won't, they will find the others who will.

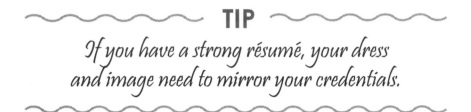

TIP

If you have a strong résumé, your dress and image need to mirror your credentials.

When acquiring clothing for your interviews and work, remember to dress two levels above the job you are seeking. In other words, dress like management, not entry level. Employers aren't looking for your fashion savvy, they want to know what you know and what you will accomplish and how you will fit in their corporate culture. They probably have enough dress and appearance problems with current staff; they don't want to compound these same problems with new hires.

You need to be consistent with your dress and appearance as you go through the interview process and to the workplace itself. Your wardrobe should be structured for the demands of your work on a moment's notice (an unannounced visit by the senior management, a last-minute business lunch, for example). More important, being prepared gives you a well-deserved return on investment.

Suit

The best colors for interviewing and transitioning into your new career are navy, black and charcoal suits. These are the colors of business. Choices include solids, stripes and patterns. Navy and black solid suits are best for mix-and-match. Stripes and patterns have to be worn only as a "nested" suit (worn together). Stripes and patterns that are used for mix-and-matching look like an outfit forced together and does not look right.

One exception, a black and white, taupe or tan hairline or micro-screen pattern looks like a fancy solid. The two colors are woven together in a screen pattern. The jacket can be matched with medium or charcoal gray, black, tan, or taupe slacks. The pant can also be worn with a black blazer if needed. It is best to keep the suit pant for the suit because a suit jacket will outlast the pant by about 2 to 1.

Non-interview suit colors are:

- □ oxford gray (light to medium shade in solids, stripes or patterns)

- □ taupe (gray/tan, medium or dark shade, in solids or muted patterns)

- □ olive (loden. brownish hue or black olive mainly solid or muted pattern)

- □ charcoal blue (shade in between navy and black, solids, stripes or patterns)

- □ brown (shading medium to dark, solids, stripes or patterns)

- □ tan (be careful in picking the shade, make sure not yellow based because you don't want to wash out or look pale, choose solids and muted patterns)

These colors round out the suit wardrobe. If you are wearing suits mostly to work, business colors concentrate on the navys, grays and black supplemented with the colors mentioned above. Only pick colors that work in your situation. Whatever you pick should enhance your overall image and consistency.

Knowing your personality type can help you choose colors that will enhance the image you want and minimize problems. If you are someone who is intimidating and overbearing, soften up your suit color so you appear friendly and approachable. Use a medium gray or a medium slate blue (mid blue/gray shade).

If you are someone who does not command respect, dress for power and authority. Dress in black, navy or charcoal colors. Buy good quality and make sure your suit fits you very well.

For someone who is a regular personality, you can dress either for power and authority or be friendly and approachable. It will depend on the interview situation and what you are trying to achieve. The guidelines also apply for work.

For interviewing, a good suit model is the three-button, single-breasted, pipe and flap pocket and non-vented coat, center vent or side vent. The non-vented model is normally cut so it fits fuller across the waist and hips. If the vent does not lie closed, the garment does not fit properly.

Suit coats cut with a center vent are normally traced at the middle or cut tighter (in other words, there is an extra dart above the lower outside coat pocket that is used to take in the coat waist). If the vent doesn't close and is split, it is a problem. An experienced tailor may be able to alter the garment if there is enough fabric, so the vent closes. If not, do not purchase this coat. Currently a number of manufacturers make a fuller fit center-vented model and the vent will close.

This jacket model will extend over the shoulder points by approximately ¾ to 1 inch, the chest piece on both sides will come almost to the center of the chest. Purchase a jacket that flows with your body and is made of pliable light-weight construction.

The second model is a two-button jacket, pipe and flap pocket, which is an alternative to the three-button. Current two-button models have a higher button stance and the lapel is not so long. These styles are available in non-vented, center vent and side vent.

Like the three-button jacket, the non-vented is a fuller fit across the waist and hips. The center vent needs to close, so try to find this model in a fuller fit. If not, a tailor may or may not have enough material to close the vent (don't purchase if you cannot close the vent).

The pant model can be a double reverse (pleat facing out to the pocket) or single reverse pleat pant (facing out to the pocket, either pleat has a more slender and balanced fit). As an alternative, a flat front pant is acceptable. Remember all three pant models should be full enough across the abdomen so the pants don't wrinkle at the lap when sitting.

Do not wear a double-breasted suit to a professional interview. It is considered too high fashion. You are there to get a job, not make a fashion statement. There is a time and place for the more elegant and dressy double-breasted models, but don't wear this during an interview.

Start with a navy or black suit to get you through the interview. If your work requires a suit once or twice a week and the rest of the week is business casual, these jackets can be mix-and-match with other slacks and shirts. If your work requires a suit 3 or more days a work, you will have to have enough suits so you aren't wearing the same suit every other day or 3 days. You have to plan to have enough suits for a 2-week rotation. We show you the best things to buy as you build your wardrobe in chapter 19.

Shirt

For the formal interview, always wear a white shirt. A superfine Pima or Egyptian cotton in a pinpoint oxford or broadcloth weave, a point collar, long sleeve barrel (button cuff), convertible (button cuff or cuff link) or French cuff (cuff folds back and you have to use cuff links). Make sure the collar point length is 2 ½ to 2 ¾ inches in length for a spread collar and 3 inches for a semi-spread or close point collar. Tie widths run approximately 3 ¾ to 4 inches in width and suit coat lapel widths are approximately 4 inches in width. It is important that the shirt collar length is long enough to match up the width of the tie and jacket lapel so everything is symmetrical.

TIP

Your shirt bridges your outfit and your tie binds it together.

The shirt collar leaf or back width needs to be at least 1 ¾ inches wide so it completely covers up the tie in the back. The front collar band should be at least 1 inch high and come up just below your "Adam's apple." You do not want your shirt too low or high on your neck, but the collar should be in good position to complement the jacket. This is important so the tie becomes the focal point to lead up to your face.

The width of the shoulders of the shirt should fit off your shoulders to allow enough room for your upper shoulders and chest. Make sure the shirt is at least 2 inches bigger than the fullest part of your chest, stomach and hips. The shirt should be long enough so it goes at least 4 to 5 inches deep inside the waist of the pant. Don't let yourself look sloppy by having your shirt come untucked when you sit down or stand up.

The cuff on the sleeve should be wide enough to slide fluidly up and down your wrist especially over a watch, as well as to allow for shrinkage. If not, it will become so tight that you won't be able to shut your cuff, whether it buttons or you use cuff links. Make sure the sleeve length is at least 1 inch longer than what the size says. For example, if the shirt is marked 16 x 35, from the center back of the neck to the end of the cuff, lay the shirt sleeve flat and measure. If it measures 36 or 36 ½, that is what you want. The manufacturer has allowed for shrinkage.

The dress shirt bridges your outfit together. Make sure the shirts you choose look like quality garments and match up well with the suit fabrics. You never want to wear a suit or a shirt that appears better than the other. You want them to complement each other. In other words, avoid buying cheaply made shirts. Empty your closets of shirts that look limp frayed (around the collar and cuff for sure) or look as if they have seen better days.

Shirt and tie combinations are very important. They say a lot about you and your image.

- Solid white (for professional interviewing – white only, and no button-down collars. Point or semi-spread are the best collar styles)

- Solid blue, ink or French blue, ecru or ivory

- White background solid with pinstripes, narrow or multi-stripes

- White background graph checks with navy, burgundy, or both

Tie

Your tie represents your creativity. It says a lot about who you are and what you are. Make sure you have a good quality silk tie. Silk is measured in mm or a good barometer is 30 to 40 ounce weight. The best silk neckwear is made in wovens (textured surface, made with two to three layers of muslin, cotton or wool), satins (lighter weight and have a shiny surface) and ancient madder (is a duller finish and has a smooth rich feel).

With a darker suit and white shirt, the more color the tie has, the better it is. The tie expresses your creativity. Your tie can be a solid, fancy solid, micro-screen, panel, or parque weave (a reverse woven square). Almost anything will work except cartoon characters, words, flames, neon or wild designs.

The more color the tie has, the better it is. It becomes the focal point of your outfit. Your tie defines your creativity; it binds your outfit together and leads to your face. Be careful to avoid ties that send the wrong message, such as bright neons, words or cartoon characters. There are "Power Ties" that you will want in your wardrobe, check our Web site for the most current version. You want to get enough ties that you are not wearing the same tie daily or even every other day. You need enough to get you through a 2-week rotation and have enough ties so you do not get tired of wearing the same ones repeatedly.

TIP

A coordinated outfit is the result you want. Clothing should lead up to your face, not down to your body.

Buy only according to your needs, and buy enough ties to allow you to mix-and-match with your shirts and suits. Sometimes just changing the tie gives you a completely different look, even if you are wearing the same suit.

When buying a tie, use these criteria before making a purchase. This is a good litmus test to use and follow:

☐ Tie is smooth, not a rumpled or wavy surface.

☐ Lined end-to-end and edge-to-edge.

☐ Smooth and soft not a stiff board. If too stiff, a good knot cannot be tied.

☐ The tie width needs to match up to the width of the coat lapel width so it is not too narrow or wide, but symmetrical and balanced.

☐ The tie should come to the top, middle or bottom of the waistband.

☐ There should never be a space below the bottom of the tie and top of the waist of the pant.

☐ Use your fingernails to scratch the front of the tie. If you get no filaments on your nails, your tie is well made and will not shed.

Belt

Belt widths are 1 inch to 1⅛ inches wide with gold or silver buckles. Buckles should be classic styling not flamboyant. No chunky buckles, please.

For the interview, the belt should be a calf, or fine quality cowhide, Kip leather with classic styling. In the interview, you are asking someone to employ you. At work, you never want to have a messy appearance. If you cannot keep your pants up with a belt, substitute a belt with braces.

LEATHER GUIDE
for Belts and Braces

☐ Aniline   ☐ Kid
☑ Kip   ☐ Deerskin
☑ Calf-skin   ☐ Lambskin
☐ Matisse   ☐ Plongé
☐ Glove   ☐ Cordovan
☐ Nubuc   Shell
☐ Suede

Your leather belt should complement your shoes and be the same color. Never mix colors. Kip or calf-skin leathers have a duller appearance. Either of these leathers is normally thicker and holds the finish better than a shiny thin leather belt.

Luxury belts such as alligator, crocodile, ostrich, lizard, snakeskin and eel are examples of luxury belts. These belts are nice but do not last as long as Kip or calf-skin. Luxury skin belts are very expensive and need to be treated with extra care when being worn. When money is not an object, these belts can be considered as an option.

Select a solid strap or embossed (textured weave) belt that is 1 to 1 ⅛ inches wide in silver, gold or brass with a silver and gold square or round buckle (keep color similar to your jewelry). Choose solid strap or strap belts in black, burgundy, brown and mid-tan.

Braces

If you cannot keep your pants up with a belt, then use good calf-skin, Kip, fine quality cowhide leather solid strap or braided braces. Leather lasts longer than rayon, silk or elastic and has a more professional look. Remember, braces button into the waistband.

Never wear a pair of clip-on suspenders. It is inappropriate for the interview and day-to-day professional dress.

Fabric braces are fine for a short period of time. The problem is these materials will eventually fray and become limp. A good pair of leather braces will last a long time. When it is time to refresh them, a good shoemaker can refinish these braces.

Use the following criteria when wearing braces:

Make sure the brace buttons are positioned properly for your abdomen. Proper positioning is important so your pants will stay where they are fitted, whether you are standing or sitting. Use this as a guide for brace button placement: In front, the brace buttons should start about 3 inches to the right and left of your navel; in back, start the buttons about 2 to 3 inches right and left center of your spine. If you have a large abdomen, place the buttons 1 inch closer to your navel in front; no need to change the back.

If your waistbands have a tendency to roll over, have a stiffening web material put inside the lining of the inside waistband to prevent this from happening. Be aware of this, because it is distracting and uncomfortable to you to sit down at an interview or work and have your waistband roll over.

When fitting your waist, make sure you keep the waistband comfortable so you can get at least one thumb in each side without having to squeeze in. By doing this you allow the braces to do their job. They will adjust the pants on your waist when you sit or stand. This keeps your pants where they need to be worn: level to the ground at the navel, hip bones on the side and the small of the back on your back waist.

Hosiery

Socks complement your outfit. They should not take away or be noticed. Socks should cover your legs when you sit down and not expose any skin. Pick fine-gauge yarns such as mercerized cottons or Merino wools rather than bulky fabrics. Make sure whatever you pick looks professional and has a quality look. You want to make sure when you put the socks on that they stay up and do not sag down.

Socks can be similar to the colors and shades that match the slacks of the garment you plan to wear. You do not have to match perfectly. Solids or small patterns are acceptable. Pattern socks add to the overall creativity of your garment – an added touch.

For your sock inventory, add colors that will complement your suits and slacks, all in over-the-calf style, fine-gauge Merino wool or cotton lisle, solid or patterns.

Wear over-the-calf socks. This length comes up to below the knee. You never want to show skin when sitting down. Quality socks, as an example, are made of 65% Merino wool and 35% nylon or mercerized cotton and nylon. In the fabric chapter, we told you that Merino wool is a lanolin-rich, soft touch strong fabric (body oil genetically embedded in the wool fibers). For socks, it is mixed with nylon to reinforce the strength and add longevity to the wear.

Socks can be solid or a small pattern. Keep your socks similar to the color of the suit. Pattern socks add another dimension of creativity similar to the tie and adds to a polished professional look. Patterns that work well can be small multi-colored square, diamond, oval and fishbone weaves.

With navy, black or charcoal suits, solid or pattern sock colors should be similar in color and shade to the suit. If it does not look right, do not wear it. Do not force something together.

Shoes

For professional interviews, wear only tie shoes, never a pair of loafers. Shoes say a lot about who and what you are. Why would you want to be casual in a formal situation? Tie shoes send the message you are stable and you know what you are doing, you present the complete package and you pay attention to the small details — you are asking to be employed, not to make a fashion statement.

TIP

Shoes last longer if you put a cedar shoe tree in your shoes every day.

Aniline or calf-skin leather shoes have a duller finish, look professional, and maintain a nice finish. Plain toe, cap toe, wing tip, slip-toe and panel styles are all good picks.

Black is the color to start with. Make sure you have at least two or three pairs. It is important to rotate shoes during the week. If you only have one pair and wear them daily, the shoes will not last long at all. Shoes have to have a break in between wearings. The leather inside needs to dry out; and that is accomplished by keeping cedar shoe trees inside. They dry out the leather inside so it does not eventually rot. Shoe trees keep the shoes blocked — the same way they were constructed.

LEATHER GUIDE
for Shoes

- ☑ Aniline
- ☐ Kid
- ☐ Kip
- ☐ Deerskin
- ☑ Calf-skin
- ☐ Lambskin
- ☐ Matisse
- ☐ Plongé
- ☐ Glove
- ☐ Cordovan
- ☐ Nubuc   Shell
- ☐ Suede

Burgundy is the second color to consider. If you are going to be wearing suits primarily to work, then burgundy is the next color to add to your shoe inventory.

Once you become employed, loafers can be added along with your tie shoes. These styles are fine for day-to-day wear, but if you have an interview or an important meeting, always defer to a tie shoe.

Plain toe, tassel and kiltie tassel are good styles for loafers. Black and burgundy are the colors of choice for your navy, black or charcoal solid, stripe and pattern suits.

Your shoes need to fit. Fit the shoe to the widest part of your foot and the widest part of the shoe. This is called the arch fit. Fit is not based on your toe length. Choose a quality aniline calf-skin leather (duller finish, not shiny; leather will maintain finish).

When going through professional interviews, only wear a black or burgundy tie shoe. For work you will find mostly tie shoes are the norm, with the exception of the dress loafer. Today most shoe manufacturers are showing predominantly tie shoes.

For comfort the best tie shoe style is the open toe blucher as opposed to a bal. (Blucher is pronounced *blue-cher*. Bal is short for *balmoral*.) The open toe blucher is woven open on the top vamp at the point where lacing of the shoe begins. This allows enough room when tying the shoes so they do not become tight across the top of your foot. The bal is closed at the point of lacing and can become tight when the shoes are tied. It is best to get shoes that have open toe blucher styles.

Accessories

Accessories such as glasses and jewelry should make no "noise." If you wear these items, you want to complement your clothing and add to your professional image.

If you wear glasses, the frames should complement the shape of your face and hairstyle. The lenses should be clear so there is nothing clouding or hiding your eyes. Frames should have some color, such as tortoise shell, so that your frames do not become monotone or blend in with your skin.

~~~ **TIP** ~~~

Do not wear too many accessories, they can be distracting. You never want to appear gaudy or try to make an individual fashion statement.

Your watch should be thin not thick, oval or square, gold or white face with a sweep hand. It is best to have a leather band because it does not fray the cuffs of the shirt or coat like metal band watches do.

If you wear a bracelet, make sure it is lightweight and tasteful – nothing heavy.

Do not wear more than one ring per hand. If you wear a lapel pin, make sure it is not large. It can represent an organization you belong to or even an American flag. You just do not want to wear a pin that is gaudy or oversized that will cause a distraction.

Outerwear

Your outerwear is often the first, and sometimes the only, article of clothing seen – it's visible at the point first impressions begin. Make sure your overcoat is a current model, in good condition, fits you well and is clean.

A good all-weather coat with a removable liner is a good item to have. It will work up to the extreme cold of winter. Microfiber is an excellent choice of fabric because it maintains its shape, doesn't wrinkle and travels well. It can be worn in a rain or snow shower. The fabric is water repellent, not waterproof. If it gets wet, it will dry out. When the weather turns warm, the liner can be removed and the coat worn as a raincoat in spring, summer and early fall months.

The best style is either a single or double-breasted 47-inch length, flat or twill finish, 100% microfiber (matted finish, not shiny and a soft supple finish not stiff), belted. The best colors are black or very dark charcoal.

An alternative to microfiber fabrics will be cotton, found in a twill or gabardine weave (woven in a diagonal mini-rope direction). Make sure you select superfine cotton, densely woven with a "silk or wet like" finish to the fabric, not a dry and coarse feel.

Cotton manufactured with care will normally hold its shape well and not look as if you slept in your coat. Khaki, tan, taupe and black are the preferred colors in a single or double-breasted belted model, 45- to 47-inch coat length.

To get year-round wear, make sure the coat has a button-in or zip-in liner (liner has sleeves), so the coat can be worn as a raincoat for spring and as an all-weather coat in the fall and winter.

When the weather is sub zero, there is no substitute for a long wool topcoat, 45 to 47 inches in length, single or double-breasted, with set-in or raglan sleeves (if selecting a raglan model, the coat can be belted as an option). There are different weights for different climates. Get a wool coat with good weight, approximately 24 ounces is heavy enough for the worst of winter's fury.

Melton, velour and lamb's wool are excellent fabric choices for any of winter's elements. It doesn't matter if these materials get wet, they will dry out.

When luxury fabrics like cashmere and camel hair get soaked, their surface can get matted down and be ruined. If you choose to purchase one of these coats, only wear when it is cold out, not wet.

Not all areas of the country have subzero weather, but can have cold days. As an alternative to the all-weather coat, there are lightweight wool topcoats made of wool gabardine or lightweight worsteds. The fabrics can weigh anywhere from 14 to 21 ounces. The materials are usually very tightly woven, superfine worsted wools. Names associated with these weights are gabardines, twills and lightweight worsted wools. The twills and gabardines are mostly available in black, taupe and khaki solids. The lightweight worsteds are found in solid colors: black, charcoal, taupe and tan; patterns include black and white salt-and-pepper, herringbone and birdseye weaves.

Types of Outerwear (you may only need one)

All-weather coats

- ☐ **Microfiber** – Black, taupe or khaki microfiber single or double-breasted with a button-in or zip-out full robe (with sleeves) liner

- ☐ **Cotton** – Black, taupe, khaki or tan single or double-breasted, belted, 45 to 47 inch length, button-in or zip-out liner (with sleeves)

Cold weather wool topcoat

- ☐ Black, navy, charcoal single or double-breasted (no belt) solid lamb's wool, melton, velour topcoat

- ☐ Black and white or gray and black lamb's wool, cheviot or saxony donegal or herringbone raglan belted wrap coat

Warm weather winter topcoats

- ☐ Black, taupe, tan or khaki, single-breasted, set-in or raglan sleeve, no belt, superfine wool worsted gabardine or twill fabric, 45 to 47 inches in length

- ☐ Black, charcoal gray, taupe or tan, single or double-breasted, lightweight worsted wool, set-in and raglan sleeve, solid and no belt

- ☐ Black and white, black and gray, salt and pepper, birdseye, or herringbone lightweight worsted wool, single-breasted, set in sleeve, 45 to 47 inches in length with no belt

9

Suits Me: Professional Dress for Women

You cannot be taken seriously if you are not dressed appropriately. Whether you like it or not, you cannot get past the notion that people will form their first impression of you, and to some extent who or what you represent, based on your dress and appearance. In a world that seems to promote that dressing down is now the "norm," I think one does so at their own professional peril. Your dress and appearance also affect the way you feel during the conduct of your business. If your appearance lacks even a moderate level of "attention to detail," your prospective new client might be thinking whether you or your firm will apply the same low level of attention to detail to their business. Is that what you want?

– Bob Sartor

Classic conservative styles resonate well with employers and fashion is a non-issue. They want to know what you know, what you can accomplish and whether you can fit into their corporate culture.

The women's wear manufacturers make all kinds of clothing. By and large it is difficult to find good professional styles that are well made. This mode of dress has been mostly abandoned. As dress in the workplace shifts away from casual and becomes more professional, manufacturers will have to focus on this growing trend.

Some Canadian, Asian and European manufacturers are offering good selections. The fabrics are pack-n-go, easy care (microfiber polyester, some are machine washable, some are wool stretch, others are dry clean), very well made and ideal for year-round wear. These garments are affordable and can be found as separates – excellent for any season and wardrobe planning.

Sizes can be found in misses, petite, women's and women's petite plus. Any woman should be able to get a good quality garment not only for the interview but for work as well.

When going through the interview process, make sure you have the right clothing to get you through all the interviews. It is the same clothing you will be wearing to work. Remember, whatever you do daily, you represent your company at meetings, conventions and most importantly working with clients.

When building a professional wardrobe for interviewing and your work, think of your wardrobe as one that will give you a return on your investment. This is the value of wardrobe planning (see chapter 19). Fashion and classic styles do not mix. You don't have to be a fuddy duddy, but dress two levels above the job you are seeking. Remember, when acquiring suits, the fabric should have good body and drape so it does not cling or break down. Avoid fabric that looks completely wrinkled five minutes after you put the garment on. Ideally, buy suit separates that allow you maximum flexibility for pack-n-go and mix-and-matching.

If the garment does not possess these attributes, pass on it. Wardrobe building, year-round wear and maximum return on investment depend on smart wardrobe planning and making good buying decisions based on your wardrobe building plan. The benefits will pay for themselves many times over.

Suit

Black, navy and charcoal are the colors of business, and these are the components of the professional woman's wardrobe. You are interviewing to gain employment in a well-paying career. The emphasis is on you, your knowledge and skills, not about your fashion sense (unless what you wear makes a horrible fashion statement).

When expanding your wardrobe colors for work, you can incorporate eggplant or raisin (dark plum), taupe, olive, red (blue based, no orange hue), petrol (charcoal turquoise), tan, charcoal brown, oxford and pearl gray.

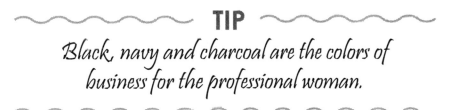

TIP

Black, navy and charcoal are the colors of business for the professional woman.

For the interview process, black and navy solids are ideal for mix-and-match and to dress up and down. Stripes and pattern suits have to be worn together. There is one exception and that is the black and white micro-screen or hairline. It is a mix of a black and white, taupe or tan thread, woven on the vertical and horizontal pattern. The jacket, like a solid black and navy, can be mixed with a charcoal, medium gray, black, taupe or tan skirt or slack.

Black and navy jackets can be mixed with taupe, tan, winter white, charcoal, oxford, pearl gray, loden and black olive skirts and pants. You can create a multitude of mix-and-match outfits for interviewing and transition these outfits for work. Eggplant or raisin, red and black olive jackets can be used for mix-and-matching.

For interviewing and work, the best styles are classic single-breasted, non-vented, pipe and flap pocket jackets in one, two, three and four button styles. The jackets should be made of a lightweight fusible so it flows and drapes to your body.

If a jacket is stiff or limp at the store, stay away from it. These types of constructions will be nothing but a nightmare. The make of these garments is cheap and will break down in dry cleaning. Tailors are not magicians. There is only so much they can do. If a garment isn't made right, it will only get worse as time goes on.

Skirts should be a mid-length, which is anywhere from three fingers above to three fingers below the knee. If you choose a longer skirt, it should come to the top of the calf. Anything longer will look dowdy or old-fashioned.

Blouse/shell

For the interview, always wear a white blouse with point, semi-spread or spread collar. Button-down styles are for less formal interviews. The blouse bridges your outfit together. Classic blouse styles are best, and plain simple models work best not only for the interview process but for professional dress as well.

Today non-iron cottons are available in blouses. These high-quality cottons launder in cold-water wash cycles, dry for about 20 minutes in a delicate permanent dryer cycle. You simply take the blouse out of the dryer and it is ready to wear. These fabrics do not break down. They look fresh all day long. It lends to an overall professional look.

You can wear a blouse, or a shell is optional. It should drape and not cling. The fabric should have good body and density so there is no see-through effect. The neck should be crew-neck styling that comes up to the base of the neck. Some of the best shells can be found in a pack-n-go microfiber. These fabrics are easy care, have a great fit and look fresh all day long. Long sleeve and short sleeve are optional styles.

Shells work great not just for interviewing but also for professional dress at work. These can be worn with or without the jacket in the office and maintain a professional appearance.

Neckwear

When interviewing, wear a necklace or string of pearls or an oblong scarf – but wear only one item. You don't want to cause any distractions around your face. You can add color with a scarf for the workday, interview or professional dress. A long narrow oblong scarf in a solid or print silk is much better than a full square style. The full square is too much material around the neck.

The more color the scarf has, it shows your creativity. The patterns can be geometric, floral or vertical panel. No cartoon characters or anything that sends the wrong message about you. A scarf stands out. When you start adding other accessories in addition to a scarf, it gets too crowded around the neck and creates distractions. Especially for interviewing, pick out one item and go with it.

If you decide to wear a necklace, make sure it is not gaudy or too heavy. The necklace should complement what you are wearing, not become the center of attention. Styling should be conservative not flamboyant.

Pearls, like any necklace, should be simple and classic, used to complement your outfit for interviewing and work. A scarf, necklace and pearls all stand on their own, each one by itself helps complete the accessories you choose for your outfits. Keep your neck accent simple.

Belts

A belt is optional. If you do choose to wear one, your belt should be a simple classic style, Kip or calf-skin leather with a duller finish, not with a high shine. Width should be from 1 to 1 1/8 inches wide. Gold, silver or brass round or square buckles are good styles for interview or professional dress. If your jewelry is a combination of silver and gold, then a combination gold and silver belt buckle will work.

Your belt should match your shoes and purse. Never mix colors, black to black, burgundy to burgundy and brown to brown. Black and burgundy are your primary colors for interviewing and professional dress.

Once you have your basics, other optional colors are red, taupe and eggplant. Just make sure you have the same matching color shoes and purses as the belt.

Purses

Choose a conservative classic style, nothing large. A small clutch style is appropriate for interviewing and professional dress. A purse is something you wear. It should be the same type of leather as your shoes and belt in calf-skin leather. It should not have a sheen – opt for a duller finish. Your purse is not a piece of luggage in which you carry everything that you have. Your purse says a lot about you. It is an extension of who you are. A smaller purse shows you are well organized.

Shoes

Your shoes should be a classic, conservative closed-toe style. Pumps should be 1 to 1 ½ inches in height. The shoes can be a plain toe, cap toe or a woven balmoral weave (circular perforated weave). No ribbons or buckles. The leather should be a calf-skin or aniline leather with a duller finish.

No open-toe pumps or strappy sandals for interviewing or professional dress. Nobody wants to see your toes. Most companies have gone back to closed-toe pumps or flats for the office.

Shoes are an extension of who and what you are. Why spend all the time putting your clothing and non-clothing items together and ruin your outfit with cheap or the wrong style shoes?

Make sure your shoes have a good finish and shine, with no holes in the soles, missing leather, cracks or peeling.

LEATHER GUIDE for Shoes

☑ Aniline   ☐ Kid
☐ Kip   ☐ Deerskin
☑ Calf-skin ☐ Lambskin
☐ Matisse   ☐ Plongé
☐ Glove   ☐ Cordovan
☐ Nubuc   Shell
☐ Suede

Polish the edges of the sole too. If your heels are worn down, take them to a shoe maker and have them replace the rubber before it is worn down to the nail.

Accessories

Accessories should complement what you are wearing and never draw attention away from you. Just imagine the horror of a woman entering an interview room wearing something garish. The worst mistake for a formal interview, for example, is to show up in a bright multi-colored loud pattern sport jacket, tight fitting blouse with the abdomen exposed, capri slack, no hose, open-toed backless shoes. Finish off this inappropriate look with gaudy hoop earrings, multiple chains and pearls, heavy noisy bracelets and multiple rings. Why bother to show up!

Pick out four or five accessories and stop. More can cause distractions.

If you wear glasses, frames should have color such as a tortoise shell, to add color to your facial area and not be monotone. Glass frames should work well with the shape of your face and hairstyle. Your eye doctor and frame fitter can make suggestions when you choose eyeglass frames.

If you wear earrings, they should be small. Studs and similar size work well. Anything large will cause a distraction.

Pick out an oblong scarf, a necklace or a strand of pearls to wear around your neck. Only pick one item for neckwear. Anything more will be too much.

For your hands, wear no more than one ring per hand. Your watch should be a good classic style that has a thin face, white or gold, with a sweep hand (no digital readouts). The watchband should be leather. Leather will not tear up the end of the cuffs of your blouses, knit tops or the sleeves of your jacket like a metal band will.

If you decide to wear a bracelet on the other wrist, it should be simple, classic, lightweight not heavy. You don't want it to make noise when your hands are on the table or you are moving about.

Lapel pins or brooches, if you choose to wear one, should be simple and small not large and gaudy.

I've already talked about suits, so here are some additional items you'll want to purchase to help you build a wonderful year-round wardrobe. You will be able to dress up or down, spend less on your clothing overall, have classic items longer and realize a huge return on investment for your clothing dollar.

Shift dress

A shift dress should be worn with a jacket. When you leave your office, make sure you put your jacket on for a professional appearance.

Coat dress

The coat dress stands on its own and does not require a jacket, but make sure the length comes down to at least three fingers below the knee to just above the calf. The fit should be comfortable, not tight, especially sitting. Closure for the dress will be a button front.

Hosiery

Never go bare legged to work. Employers expect dress decorum to be kept. It is best to have neutral hose so you don't draw attention below your hemline. Black, navy and white hose are a fashion statement and not appropriate for work.

Shoes

Never wear a "spike heel" over 1½ inches in height. You risk developing back problems. Heel height should range from 1 to 1½ inches. Choose plain or cap closed toe pumps in various colors.

Belts

A belt is optional. If you choose to wear one, it should match your shoes. Never mix colors.

Outerwear

Outerwear that is the latest trend or color is here today and gone tomorrow. Choose classic outerwear that adds to your credibility and does not detract from it. It is the first article of clothing seen and often helps to form a person's first impression about you.

Outerwear is used for two types of weather. One is cold, wet and damp. The other is subzero, dry, sleet, freezing rain or snow. An all-weather coat is ideal for the first season of cold, wet and damp. If you select your coat with a removable liner, it helps you work up to the extreme cold of winter.

Microfiber is an excellent choice of fabric because it maintains its shape, doesn't wrinkle and travels well. It can be worn in rain or snow. The fabric is water repellent, not waterproof; if it gets wet, it will dry out. When the weather turns warm, the liner can be removed and the coat can be worn as a raincoat in spring, summer and early fall months.

The best style is either a single or double-breasted 47 inch length, flat or twill finish, 100% microfiber (matte finish, and a supple feel), belted. The best colors are black or a dark charcoal. Alternative colors include taupe, khaki, mocha, cement or stone.

An alternative to microfiber fabrics will be cotton, found in a twill or gabardine weave (woven in a diagonal mini-rope direction). Make sure you select a superfine cotton, densely woven that has a "silk or wet like" finish to the fabric, not a dry and coarse feel.

Cotton manufactured like this will normally hold its shape well and will not easily wrinkle. Khaki, tan, taupe and black are the preferred colors in a single or double-breasted belted, 45 to 47 inch coat length.

For year-round wear, make sure the coat has a button-in or zip-out liner (liner has sleeves), so the coat can be worn as a rain coat for spring and as an all-weather coat in the fall and winter.

When the weather is subzero, there is no substitute for a long wool topcoat, 45 to 47 inches in length, single or double-breasted, set-in or raglan sleeve (if selecting a raglan model, the coat can be belted as an option). There are different weights for different climates. Get a wool coat with good weight of approximately 24 ounces, heavy enough for the worst of winter's fury.

Melton, velour and lamb's wool are also excellent fabric choices for any of winter's elements. It doesn't matter if these materials get wet, they will dry out. Luxury fibers such as camel hair and cashmere can get ruined if they get water on them. If the fabric gets soaked, the surface can get matted down and is virtually impossible to revitalize. If you choose to purchase camel hair or cashmere, wear it only when it is cold out, not wet.

Not all areas of the country have subzero weather, but can have cold days. As an alternative to the all-weather coat, there are lightweight topcoats made of wool gabardine or wool twills. These fabrics can weigh anywhere from 14 to 21 ounces and are usually very tightly woven superfine worsted wools.

The twills and gabardines are most commonly available in black, taupe and khaki solids. Other colors include navy, charcoal, mocha, stone and red. Patterns include black and white, gray and black in salt-and-pepper, herringbone and birdseye weaves.

Types of Outerwear (you may only need one)

All-weather coats

- ☐ **Microfiber** – Black, taupe or khaki microfiber single or double-breasted with a button-in or zip-out full robe (with sleeves) liner

- ☐ **Cotton** – Black, taupe, khaki or tan single or double-breasted, belted, 45 to 47 inch length, button-in or zip-out liner (with sleeves)

Cold weather wool topcoats

- ☐ Black, navy, charcoal single or double-breasted (belt optional) solid lamb's wool, melton, velour topcoat

- ☐ Black and white or gray and black lamb's wool, cheviot or saxony Donegal or herringbone raglan belted wrap coat

Warm weather winter topcoats

- ☐ Black, taupe, tan or khaki, single-breasted, set-in or raglan sleeve, no belt, superfine wool worsted gabardine or twill fabric, 45 to 47 inches in length

- ☐ Black, charcoal gray, taupe or tan, single or double-breasted, lightweight worsted wool, set-in and raglan sleeve, solid and belt optional

- ☐ Black and white, black and gray, salt and pepper, birdseye, or herringbone lightweight worsted wool, single-breasted, set in sleeve, 45 to 47 inches in length with belt optional

In general, choose fabric that suits you year round, such as 100% wool worsted, two-ply weave, and 9 to 10 ounces in weight. Look for garments that are Teflon coated, natural stretch, stain and wrinkle-resistant.

There are wool/polyester blend fabrics available, but keep in mind these fabrics will not last as long as pure wool. Polyester is a manmade synthetic and over time will break down and start to ball or peel. This doesn't happen to wool. Quality lasts – and over time, more expensive garments pay for themselves.

10

Dressing Down: Business Casual Dress for Men

Business casual is the scariest thing I have ever put in my company policy manual. It was improperly handled by my human resources department, who didn't set rules and ultimately it tore through my company image, my employees' morale and the overall vision of my company. Now this book is my company dress code manual. We give it to every employee and expect them to adhere to it. Period.

– Doug N., Online Entrepreneur

When the interview or work setting is less formal than professional and no tie or scarf is required, business casual attire is fitting. Business casual is often referred to as bridge dressing. Often only a half-step down from professional or formal, it is by no means casual. Business casual is the dressing up of casual, this level of apparel fits in between.

Business casual maintains professional appearance in a less formal environment. Not all work situations call for formal dress, but they do still require professionalism. Business casual dress is not sloppy dress – that does not work for most firms or their clients.

Business casual dress adapts to most situations especially when unexpected clients show up or when out of the office meetings are called on a moment's notice. Business casual allows a man or woman to dress appropriately for most situations.

Fabric is often the start of successful business casual dress; the fabrics drape, do not cling, fit well and are symmetrical to your body's shape. Not only does a top and bottom work well together, they also work with a coordinated blazer or sport coat to complete a polished outfit.

Core Business Casual Wardrobe

Sport coat or blazer

If you do not already have a navy or black suit from which the jacket can double as a blazer, then purchase either a suit or a blazer. Blazers are not the only jackets for business casual. A nondescript patterned sport coat is another very popular item.

Navy and black are the most basic foundation of any wardrobe. Today's fabrics are high performance stretch wools that are pack-n-go fabrics and wrinkle and stain resistant. These jackets look as fresh at the end of day as in the morning. Textured weaves such as gabardine, high twist, serge or faille cloth are ideal for blazers as they give the fabric a unique polished look.

What's the Difference Between a Blazer and a Sport Coat?

A blazer is a solid color often made with a plastic, horn, gold, silver, brass solid or embossed metal button. Black or navy hard plastic or horn buttons are often preferred over metal. Most people do not want their buttons noticed.

The sport coat is made in some kind of a pattern. It can be bold or subtle. The use of several colors and plastic or horn buttons will complement the dominant color of the pattern.

Either coat is used in business casual dress; either one can add credibility to your outfit. Even though a tie isn't required, it is optional (ideal for dress up or down on a moment's notice), and a tie completes any outfit for an unexpected meeting or client.

With business casual dress, the jacket is the bridge to a professional and polished look. When an interview is business casual, it is best to use a blazer or sport coat because either sends out a professional message about you. For either work or an interview, you'll be prepared. Remember, it is better to be overdressed than underdressed. Here's what to look for:

- ☐ Black or navy super 100's, 110's, 120's, 140's, or 150's threads per square inch (TSI) Merino worsted wool gabardine, high twist, serge or faille, two or three-button blazer, either center, side or non-vented style

- ☐ Sport coat in a 100's, 110's, 120's, 140's, or 150's (TSI) Merino worsted wool micro-screen, salt and pepper weave, tic weave, birdseye or a muted-pattern. Either two or three-button jackets in center, side or non-vent models.

Patterns of multiple colors allow maximum mix-and-match with pants, shirts and knits. These color combinations are adaptable:

- ☐ olive/tan/black
- ☐ taupe/black/blue
- ☐ gray/black/blue
- ☐ tan/black/blue
- ☐ olive/taupe/black

Slacks

Fabrics you choose should be year round in weight and wrinkle and stain resistant. For maximum comfort, try to get stretch combined in the weave of your slacks. It helps to repel wrinkles, while draping nicely so pants do not cling to your body.

Choices include Merino superfine wools, 9 to 10 ounce year-round weight, two-ply weave, 100's to 150's TSI (how many threads per square inch.). Higher quality wools have a silky, wet-like feel rather than coarse or dry to the touch. Other good choices include microfiber and Tencel for business casual slacks.

The best slack models include pleated (pleats face out to the pockets to give a slimming appearance) and flat front. If you choose a flat front, make sure it fits as full as a pleat. If not, your pants will have a tendency to wrinkle across your lap when you sit.

Shirts

Business casual really just means "tie not required." Even though this mode of dress is more relaxed, it is no less professional. If you choose fabrics that need to be pressed, make sure they are pressed; anything less is not acceptable. Business casual is not a license for a sloppy appearance.

Non-iron cotton shirts are available not only in dress models but also in solid or pattern long and short sleeve styles. These fabrics look as great at the end of the day as in the morning. Pinpoint, poplin and twills are offered in non-iron cotton business casual shirts. The technology is easy care: wash, dry and wear. With little maintenance, the fabrics look great throughout the day and wear well through multiple launderings.

Collar styles are point, spread, button down and hidden button down. Any of these models work well for business casual and can be worn with or without a sport coat or blazer.

Polo styles are acceptable as an alternative. The most popular fabrics are mercerized or pique in a fine Pima or Egyptian two-ply cotton weave. These are a fine high count weave, available in solid or muted patterns. New technology has developed a non-iron easy care cotton pique. The wash, dry and wear fabric acts just like the regular non-iron cotton dress or casual shirts.

Basic shirts you should own in non-iron cotton are twill, poplin or pinpoint in a point, hidden or button down collar in solid white, blue and ecru. Optional colors are jewel tones, taupe, khaki, gold, cocoa, brick, black, navy, sage, rose, slate blue, silver, charcoal, melon and apple green.

Knits

Often referred to as soft tops, knits can be found in silk, cotton, microfiber, fine-gauge Merino wool or in a combination of acrylic and modal (viscose or rayon). Collar styles offered will be with a crew or mock neck, polo – a three-button placket with a lay down collar or turtleneck. Preferred models are mock and lay down collar styles.

These tops go great under a jacket or with a pair of slacks and have a professional polished appearance. These styles are accepted for business casual as an alternative to a shirt. Examples of acceptable colors in polo, mock or crew styles are ivory, tan, taupe, black, olive, ink blue, charcoal, or mélange mixes in ivory/black, tan/black or charcoal/black.

Knits can be found in short or long sleeve styles, in solid or fancy mélange weaves with twisted yarns for a multi-colored look. The more colors in the knit will add to how many items you can mix-and-match with.

Belts

The styles in business casual are not much different than styles for professional dress. Although the dress is not as formal, the message you send is not any less professional. Belts and braces are used for professional transition to business casual dress.

Your leather belt should complement your shoes and be the same color. Do not mix the colors of your shoes and belt.

Choose a solid strap or embossed (textured weave), 1 to 1 ⅛ inch in width, silver, gold, brass or silver and gold square or round buckle (keep color similar to your jewelry), in black, burgundy, brown or mid-tan.

Braces

Braces are acceptable with business casual dress, with or without a jacket. See leather in chapter 7 for information on choosing braces.

Hosiery

Socks used for business casual are the same used for professional dress. The difference may be more use of pattern socks with business casual outfits.

Socks should complement your outfit. They should not take away or be overly noticeable. Socks should cover your legs when you sit down and not expose any skin. Pick fine-gauge yarns such as mercerized cottons or Merino wools. Make sure whatever you purchase has a quality look and feel, and a fit that keeps them in place with no sagging or slipping.

Socks should be similar to the colors and shades of the slacks or garment you plan to wear. You do not have to match perfectly. Solids or small patterns are acceptable and add to the overall creativity of your garment – an added touch.

For your sock inventory, add these colors, all in over-the-calf style or slack length style (comes up higher than ankle length), fine-gauge Merino wool or cotton lisle:

□ Solids in black, navy, charcoal, olive taupe, medium to dark brown, oxford or medium gray, tan, charcoal blue

□ Patterns in black, olive, taupe, tan, charcoal blue, navy, charcoal

Shoes

When you are dressing business casual, it is not any less professional. Although not as formal, you have a choice of shoe styles. The examples cited are not much different from what is worn for professional, except that wing tips are not recommended. This style is out of place for business casual wear.

When you spend so much time putting everything together, the same effort and attention needs to be spent on your footwear in business casual. Select good quality aniline or calf-skin leather with a dull finish, not shiny; good leather will maintain finish.

When going through a business casual interview, your shoes can be a tie or dress slip-on style shoe. For work you will find mostly tie shoes are the norm, with the exception of the dress loafer.

For comfort the best tie shoe styles are the open toe blucher as opposed to a bal oxford. The bal is closed at the point of lacing and can become tight when the shoes are tied. The open toe blucher is woven open on the top vamp at the point where lacing of the shoe begins. This allows enough room when tying the shoes so they don't become tight across the top of your foot.

Black, burgundy, brown and mid-tan are the colors of business and professional dress.

Slip ons: Black, burgundy, mid-tan, brown (walnut or dark brown)
- ☐ Pair plain toe moccasin with a tassel
- ☐ Pair with a kiltie and tassel wing-tip style
- ☐ Pair plain toe moccasin with a penny strap
- ☐ Pair plain toe with a lap over strap with a buckle

Tie shoes: Black, burgundy, mid-tan
- ☐ Plain or cap toe style 3 to 5-eyelet blucher
- ☐ Plain toe double panel 3 to 5 eyelet blucher
- ☐ Split toe plain style 3 to 5-eyelet blucher

Tan can be worn with navy, black, medium gray, charcoal, olive (black olive or loden shades), taupe, tan and medium and dark brown solids, patterns and stripes. Make sure you do not mix other colors of belts or braces (match to the color of the shoes).

Brown (walnut or dark brown) shoes should be worn with any medium to dark brown, taupe or solid or pattern suit; do not wear with navy, charcoal or black.

Don't force colors to go together. Do not mix belts or braces, match them to the shoes.

Outerwear

If you wear a sport coat or blazer, make sure your outerwear is long enough to cover your jacket entirely. Never let your jacket stick out below your outerwear. Outerwear you select should be able to dress up or down and go with most items in your business causal wardrobe.

Depending on where you live and work and where you travel, you have a choice of wearing your topcoat or all-weather coat. The lengths of these styles will come to below mid-thigh or go approximately 3 to 6 inches below the knee. You can also wear a good quality fingertip length jacket made of leather, shearling, wool or microfiber.

These style jackets work well whether you are wearing a sport coat or blazer or not. You don't want to wear the wrong outerwear (such as a parka or a ski jacket). Your outerwear is just as important as your other clothes. Purchase a coat with a removable liner so you are not limited to the season.

☐ Solid black, charcoal or black olive in Merino wool fingertip length, single-breasted zip or button front with a fill or removable liner. Additional color choices include taupe, tan and cocoa in solid, mélange, birdseye or herringbone weaves.

☐ Black leather plongé, lambskin (removable liners for leathers allow for fall, winter and spring wear). Shearling (permanent liner for late fall and winter wear only) fingertip length, button front, shearling, permanent lining (for winter wear only), removable liner (for leather coats, for fall and early spring wear). Brown and mid-tan are other color choices to consider.

☐ Black or charcoal, cotton or microfiber shell, fingertip length, removable liner, zip or button front.

11

Dressing Down: Business Casual Dress for Women

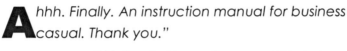

"Ahhh. Finally. An instruction manual for business casual. Thank you."

– Trish Ready, Human Resources Manager

Women have a challenge with business casual. Why? Because most women's clothing manufacturers are concerned with the latest fashions, fads and trends. Dressing well is not about exploiting your body to show skin or curves   it's about classic styling that allows for mixing and matching, and looking great in every situation.

Classic styles with a long shelf life have all but been abandoned for women. Business casual is not much different than professional dress; it may be more relaxed, but it is no less professional.

Employers are not looking for the latest capris. They are looking for people who exhibit and enhance their organizational objectives and image.

Ask Yourself These Questions:

- ☐ What is my typical day?
- ☐ What is the unexpected event during the day that I haven't planned on?
- ☐ How much travel do I do now and will it increase or decrease?
- ☐ When I meet with company clients, what image do I want to create?

These are answers you need to know before you buy anything. It is not about your personal fashion sense, it is what is going to be appropriate for the image you want, with no barriers. Firms have enough challenges with dress and appearance issues, don't add yourself to that list. A firm that chooses business casual as their dress code is often looking for a casual, open atmosphere, not a sloppy one.

Business casual has to make the same statement as professional dress, so when the call is to dress down, this is the way to approach it.

Choose garments that are made of all season fabrics and are good for pack-n-go and easy care. Look for items that are classic in design – the clothing items don't have to be stodgy – you can show your creativity by choosing cutting edge fabrics and colors. You want your clothing to have shelf life and last more than a season, and you want clothes that will mix-and-match with wardrobe additions. This is called wardrobe planning (covered in greater depth in the last chapter of this book).

Jackets

To get started, make sure navy or black suit separate jackets or blazers are included in building your business casual wardrobe. Purchase fabrics that are pack-n-go and easy care, microfiber and stretch wool that are stain and wrinkle-resistant.

Nondescript, micro-screen or muted patterns made of high performance wool or a high performance wool and silk combination are good examples of alternative style jackets.

The difference between a blazer and a suit jacket: A blazer can be accented with metal, plastic or horn buttons. Fabric and design should go with many tops and bottoms. On the other hand, a suit jacket is made of the identical fabric used for the slack or skirt. Some suit materials lend the suit coat for mix-and-match. Suit fabrics used for certain suits cannot mix-and-match, and these are called "nested."

Classic styles and colors work best, they don't get dated, don't draw unwanted attention and fit well. The most versatile jacket styles are one-, two- or three-button, single-breasted, and non-vented, with notch lapel and lower pockets that are piped or have a raised seam above the flap. Pocket flaps can be worn out or tucked in. When tucked in, it's called a besom pocket. A notch lapel is cut at the point where the collar and lapel are seamed together. You might see shawl lapels on one-button jackets, and those are acceptable too.

Choose jackets in microfiber or high performance wool tricotine, high twist or striated, gabardine, serge or faille.

In classic styles, the jacket length should be 25 to 28 inches so it comes to upper-thigh and covers the seat.

The more color in the pattern, the more mix-and-match capability you have. The most flexible patterns have the following color combinations blue/black/gray, taupe/black/olive and tan/navy/olive. Whether you are choosing a solid or a small pattern, try to find these colors:

- Solid fabrics in black solid and navy. Other optional blazer colors are taupe, red, ivory, eggplant or dark olive

- Nondescript or muted pattern, single-breasted, one-, two- or three-button jacket in a high performance stretch wool and pack-n-go and easy care microfiber in one of the following combinations in blue/black/gray, taupe/black/olive and tan/navy/olive

Skirts/slacks

When dress is business casual, either skirts or slacks are acceptable, but slacks need to be professional in appearance. Fabrics should be pack-n-go and easy care with some form of stretch, stain and wrinkle resistance. The best fabrics are high performance wool, wool and Lycra, microfiber, microfiber/rayon/Lycra combinations and Tencel/microfiber because they fit and travel well and maintain their shape.

Preferred slack models are flat fronts, single reverse and double reverse pleat pants. Some waistbands come with side elastic in the waist to provide additional comfort. Flat front slacks should fit similar to pleated models, but allow a full enough fit so that they don't wrinkle across the lap when sitting. Wrinkling undermines your appearance.

Both flat front or a pleated slack models can be dressed up or down with your choice of a blazer, sport jacket, sweater, knit top or a variety of different blouses and shells.

If you choose to wear skirts, select skirts that are mid-length that come to just above or below the knee or slightly longer styles that come to just above the calf. A straight skirt style with one front and two back panels and a back kick pleat is an excellent choice.

With skirts, you have the same flexibility as with slacks to dress up or down. You can pair either with a matching or contrasting blazer, sport jacket, assorted knits and shells and blouses.

Slacks

- ☐ Choose solid black or navy slacks in a high performance wool or microfiber flat front or pleated model. Make sure the fabric is year round, pack-n-go and easy care.

- ☐ Solid charcoal, taupe, tan, black olive or mocha solid slacks, made in high performance wool or microfiber flat front or pleated model. Make sure the fabric is year round and pack-n-go. These colors are good for mix-and-match. Consider several from this group.

- ☐ Fancy or nondescript pattern slack, the best choices include a black and gray donegal, herringbone or birdseye pattern in a high performance wool or microfiber fabric.

Skirts

☐ Solid black, navy, charcoal, taupe, tan or black olive skirt, made either of a high performance wool or microfiber, mid-length or longer length (measures to back of the calf). Can be darted or with soft tucks and with or without side waist elastic. If you choose to wear a skirt, have several of these different colors ideal for mix-and-match with sport jackets, sweaters, knits, shells or blouses.

☐ Muted or nondescript pattern skirt. Black and white, black and taupe, black and gray, black and navy, navy and charcoal and navy and taupe are color examples woven in tic, micro-screen, birdseye and salt and pepper weaves. These are excellent examples of patterns that mix-and-match with sport jackets, sweaters, knits, shells and blouses.

Blouses/shells

Blouses and shells help you create a flexible wardrobe. They should have a professional look, fit well, should not define shapes and curves and be long enough to cover the abdomen with no skin exposed.

Where available, choose non-iron cotton pinpoint oxford or poplin cotton fabrics for easy care. These blouses maintain their shape all day long. Collar styles include button down, point, close and spread. Some blouses come as a button, convertible (button cuff or cuff link), and French cuff (cuff links only).

Blouses can be solids, patterns or stripes. Business casual affords the opportunity to wear more than just white; you can easily pair blue, ink blue, rose, ecru, yellow, apple green, taupe, khaki, olive, pink, black, silver or burgundy with your blazers and jackets.

If you choose a stripe or pattern blouse, try to find white backgrounds that will be easier to mix-and-match with other wardrobe items. Depending on the season, you will find both subtle and bold color combinations in small, medium or wide stripes or multi-stripe blouses, in vertical and diagonal designs.

Shells are great alternatives to collared blouses. The best style is a jewel or crew-neck that sits at the base of the neck without a collar. Solids are easier to work with because patterns can be difficult to mix-and-match. When selecting pattern shells, make sure the colors will work with your different slacks, skirts and jackets.

Blouses

- ☐ Solid non-iron cotton or microfiber blue, pink, ecru, taupe, khaki, deep blue (ink), rose, silver, charcoal, melon, apple green and gold. Long sleeve, button cuffs and point collar styles are the best professional models. These styles are easy to mix-and-match with other components of your wardrobe.

- ☐ White ground pin or tape stripe, blue, red, charcoal, navy, green or rose. Long sleeve, button cuffs and point collar styles. Excellent for mix-and-match with other components of your wardrobe. Select non-iron cotton fabrics, so your blouse looks fresh all day long.

- ☐ Pattern white ground tattersall or window pane pattern, long sleeve, button cuff blouses. More colors in the blouse will allow more mix-and-match capabilities.

- ☐ Solid shell in long-sleeve, flat weave, crew-neck in ivory, black, navy, red, taupe, pink, eggplant, ink blue and olive. Microfiber is an outstanding choice of fabric because it is easy care, pack-n-go, holds its shape all day long and doesn't cling. Short sleeve styles are available and best worn underneath a blazer or sport jacket. Although other fabrics are available, microfiber would be the primary choice.

Knits

Made of fine-gauge wool, silk, silk/wool, acrylic, acrylic/cotton are excellent examples of knits that have a professional look, drape well to the body, and are excellent for mix-and-match.

Solid colors such as ivory, black, charcoal, taupe, red, mocha and eggplant are excellent for mix-and-match with jackets, skirts and slacks. There are fancy nondescript patterns called mélanges, in which two or three yarns are mixed together: black and ivory, black and taupe, mocha and tan are just some of many examples.

Preferred models are high V-neck, jewel, crew or mock neck, long sleeve, knitted cuff and bottom. These garments stand alone and work well underneath a jacket or sweater.

- Solid ivory, black, charcoal, taupe, red, mocha, eggplant, olive, soft yellow, rose, pink, slate blue and navy long-sleeve mock, jewel, high V-neck or crew-neck. Consider having more than one of these popular knits – good for mix-and-match.

- Nondescript/marled or mélange pattern in an ivory/black, tan/black, gray/black, brick/tan, olive/tan, blue/black, burgundy/black and burgundy/tan. These are just a few of the many combinations available. Mock, jewel, high V-neck or crew-neck style knits are available in a flat knit weave.

Sweaters

Sweaters should never fit tight or show your shape or curves. They should be as professional in appearance as a sport jacket. Longer cardigan styles (that cover the seat), zip or button fronts will work in place of a jacket. Choose solid ribbed or flat weaves made of silk, wool, silk and wool, fine-gauge cotton, acrylic and wool, and acrylic and silk. Cashmere and camel hair are luxury fibers and will not hold up to rigorous office wear. Wear these for special occasions.

Collar styles for pullovers are a high V-neck, crew or boat neck. Cardigan sweaters come in mandarin or laydown collar, button front or zip in a flat or ribbed weave. Blouses, shells or knits can all be worn underneath a sweater and paired with either a skirt or slacks. If you select pullover sweater styles, make sure the fit drapes nicely and does not cling.

Good quality sweaters are expensive, although there are a lot of cheap versions in the market. You get what you pay for. Merino or lamb's wool fine-gauge weaves are a good value, because sweaters made with these materials hold their shape and last a long time.

- ☐ Solid long cardigan, button or zip front, ribbed or flat weave, cotton, wool or silk and wool in black, navy, ivory, taupe, olive, soft yellow, rose, pink and chocolate

- ☐ Solid long sleeve or three-quarter sleeve, pullover, high V-neck, crew or boat neck, cotton, silk and wool, Merino, or lamb's wool, ribbed or flat weave in black, ivory, taupe, tan, navy, salmon, soft yellow, rose, pink, olive, navy or slate blue

Belts

Belts are optional. If you choose to wear one, it is one of the most important items you wear for business casual. Belts help complete your outfit, so always match the color to your shoes and purse. Never mix colors.

You have the choice of wearing solid straps or embossed leathers that look like exotic skins. Buy well-made leather belts such as calfskin or Kip leathers. These leathers hold their shape and finish and can be refinished after extensive wear. Good leather lasts a long time. With proper care, your good belts will remain an integral part of your belt wardrobe.

Exotic skins are expensive and require special care. If money is not an object, your choices include ostrich, snakeskin, alligator, crocodile and lizard.

Use these belts to transition from professional to business casual. Belts should be ¾ to 1 ½ inches in width, round or square, brass, gold, silver or a combination of gold and silver with a round or square buckle. Buy belts in black, burgundy, brown, mid-tan, red, navy, winter white and raisin in solid or embossed styles.

Hosiery

You can wear either socks or panty hose with slacks. Pick solid or small pattern styles, matching the color similar to the slacks. Length should be high enough not to expose your skin when sitting.

When choosing socks, it is best to make sure you are getting a good blend of fine-gauge cotton lisle or Merino wool.: 75/25, 65/35 or 80/20 in Merino/nylon or mercerized cotton lisle/nylon. This blend maintains the shape and helps keep shrinkage to a minimum. Choose quality socks in ribbed or flat weaves that stay up to cover your skin and do not bunch or slide down.

When you wear a skirt, do not go bare legged. It is best to wear a neutral panty hose so you do not draw attention below your hem line. Business is not about trends or fashion. Do not wear white, navy or black hose because they will draw attention to your legs.

- ☐ Solid black, charcoal, navy, taupe, tan or olive, Merino or cotton lisle, ribbed, slack-length socks

- ☐ Nondescript pattern black, charcoal, navy, taupe, tan or olive, Merino or cotton lisle, flat knit weave, slack length socks

Shoes

Shoes say a lot about who you are. Business casual shoes need to look professional and not follow the latest fashion trend. Above all, they need to be comfortable and fit properly. Open-toed shoes and sandals are not acceptable in the workplace.

TIP

No exposed toes, no bare legs at work.

Recommended leathers for shoes are calf-skin, aniline or Nubuc (suede appearance). They will not lose their finish, and the skins won't peel. If money is not an object, your choices can include alligator, crocodile, lizard, snakeskin, ostrich, eel, deer, buffalo and elk skin.

Black, burgundy and mid-tan are good colors to start with. Once you have your basics, you can add taupe, navy, red and chocolate. These colors will help round out your wardrobe. All these colors look professional and are versatile for mix-and-match.

Pumps

Choose pumps made of calf-skin, aniline, or Nubuc (suede appearance), solid or embossed, plain toe, cap toe or with a woven surface and heel height of 1 to 1 ½ inches. Recommended soles can be a combination leather and vibram or rubber. These shoes can be worn with either skirts or slacks.

∼∼∼∼∼∼∼ — TERM — ∼∼∼∼∼∼∼

Vibram: is a registered trademark of one of the most durable and lightweight rubber soles used for dress, casual, outdoor shoes and boots.

Black pumps with a combination or rubber sole, heel height 1 to 1 ½ inches, calf-skin, aniline, or Nubuc leather skins. The aniline or calf-skin leather can be solid or embossed. Have at least two pairs of black shoes, even three pairs, so you can rotate during the week. This practice will help keep your shoes longer without wearing out.

- ☐ Burgundy, mid-tan, taupe, navy and red with a combination or rubber sole, heel height 1 to 1 ½ inches, calf-skin or aniline leather, solid or embossed
- ☐ Chocolate Nubuc, heel height 1 to 1 ½ inches with a combination or rubber sole

Loafers

Loafers that are flat and without ribbons or metal decoration, plain or cap toe are good styles for your business casual wardrobe. Aniline or calf-skin leather, solid or embossed. This type of leather has no limit to what you can coordinate it with.

- ☐ Black, plain or cap toe, solid or embossed leather, no ribbons or metal decoration, flat, combination or rubber sole. Get at least two pair or more, so you can rotate through the week so you don't wear your shoes out quickly. Choose calf-skin or aniline leather.

- □ Mid-tan, burgundy, navy, taupe and red, solid or embossed leather, combination or rubber sole and flat not thick soles

- □ Chocolate Nubuc, combination or rubber sole, plain toe flat

Tie shoes

Tie shoes are excellent for slacks. Choose calf-skin, aniline, Nubuc, solid, plain or cap toe, vibram and leather combinations or rubber sole. These shoes are comfortable especially if you have to be on your feet during the day.

- □ Black plain or cap toe, combination or vibram sole

- □ Mid-tan, burgundy or brown, plain or cap toe, combination or vibram sole

- □ Black, brown or tan Nubuc plain toe, combination or vibram sole

Outerwear

Long coats purchased for professional dress can be transitioned for business casual. In addition to long coats, business casual wardrobes can include fingertip and pant coat length. These shorter style coats are to be worn with pants only. Their length is usually mid-thigh or just above the knee.

Microfiber, cotton, wool, shearling, leather and micro-suede are all good choices for business casual wear. These fabrics all look professional, are durable and enhance your business casual look. If money is not an object, cashmere, camel hair, mohair and angora can be considered. Be cautious not to wear these fabrics during winter's worst wet days. Once these fabrics get soaked, they can be ruined. Wear these luxury fibers only when it is cold and dry outside.

- □ Cotton, twill, gabardine or peachface, fingertip length, zip or button front and removable liner. Black and tan are primary colors to consider. Other colors can include olive, mocha, navy, taupe, stone and cement.

- □ Microfiber, fingertip or pant coat (just above or below the knee), button front, removable liner. The most versatile colors are black, charcoal, taupe, tan and stone, but you can consider eggplant, olive, rose and steel blue as alternative colors. These shades should be deep tones to give good contrast with your business casual apparel.

☐ Merino or lamb's wool, solid, mélange, birdseye or herringbone weave, fingertip or pant coat length and button front style. Choose a coat with a removable liner if available. Black, charcoal, olive, taupe, tan, navy and red are excellent choices for a solid color. For mélange, birdseye and herringbone weaves, select black and white, black and gray, black and olive, black and tan, black and taupe and taupe and oatmeal.

☐ Micro suede solid, fingertip or pant coat length and button front, with a removable liner, if available. Black, tan and taupe are excellent colors. Alternates are slate, rose, cement and green. Make sure the shades are good jewel tones and complement your business casual attire.

☐ Leather or shearling, fingertip, pant coat or full length, shearling permanent lining and leather removable liner (transition leather coat wear for the different seasons) and button or zip front. If you choose leather, choose a good lamb or calf-skin. Make sure leathers are thick enough yet supple to your touch. Stay away from leather that is stiff or thin. A good leather or shearling will last for years.

～～～ TERM ～～～

Peachface: has a very soft feel to the fabric; feels good when you touch the garment.

12

No Jacket: Casual Dress for Men

Five years ago, I attended an Air Force transition program where Dick Lerner presents a wardrobe workshop. Since then, I not only secured a job, but several subsequent promotions. Having spent 20 years wearing an Air Force uniform, not having to worry about what to wear, I know now that it does matter how you dress!
– Jim Owen, Muscular Dystrophy Association

Casual dress doesn't mean blue jeans, untucked shirt and t-shirt, despite what the term *casual* sounds like. In business, casual dress does not mean sloppy. You still need to look professional and be consistent with it. Whether it is for the interview or work, you need to send the same message about yourself you send when you dress in formal professional attire. Your message is this: "I care how I look and how others see me."

Dress like the big fish, even when dressing casually. Too many people think their ability is more important than their image – but they go together. This is how you are perceived. Even in casual situations, first impressions are lasting impressions. Don't damage your intent by being too casual. If you do not sweat the small details with even your casual dress, you will be perceived as sloppy, lax in details and perhaps in your work. Can you afford this perception? No. Nobody can.

With casual dress, jackets and ties are not required; what you wear on the top and on the bottom can stand on their own as an outfit. When a jacket is not worn, everything you wear is exposed. Casual items must fit properly and not cling nor hang too large, and should be able to mix-and-match with other components of your wardrobe.

Casual wear is evolving. While some exceptions exist for certain companies and in certain parts of the country, for the most part, casual dress no longer means polos and jeans.

Choices include tops and bottoms made of fabrics that stretch, are easy care, non-iron, wrinkle and stain resistant. Tops include casual shirts, solids and patterns, knits that have a collar or can be a crew or a mock neck and long- or short-sleeve; depending on the season.

Slacks include fabric choices of high performance stretch wool, microfiber, non-iron cotton and tencel. Most of these fabrics are easy care and pack-n-go. Their appearance stays fresh all day long.

Yours socks, shoes and belts highlight your outfits and give a polished, balanced all around look to your outfit.

Spring/summer tops

Short-sleeve polo

☐ Solid non-iron cotton pique polo white, black, ecru, navy, ink blue, denim blue, apple green, yellow, silver melon and rose are good colors that will mix-and-match. Also good to go with slacks are black, navy, taupe, tan, olive, oxford gray, charcoal gray, chino, stone and sand. A good style for this type of polo is an open sleeve and shirt bottom, not knitted.

☐ Fancy or nondescript (mélange or marled) pattern mercerized or Pima cotton short sleeve polo, open sleeve and bottom. Possible color combinations include black/ ivory, black/blue/gray, taupe/blue/black, ivory/taupe/brick, olive/ivory/black and olive/ivory/taupe. The more color combinations in the top will allow you to make and combine more outfits.

Cut and sewn short-sleeve shirt

☐ Solid twill non-iron cotton short sleeve, collared (point collar, hidden or button down), button front and open sleeve. Color choices include black, white, ecru, rose, navy, blue, denim blue, melon, olive, sage, yellow, charcoal and silver.

☐ Muted pattern non-iron cotton short sleeve, collared (point collar, hidden or button down), button front and open sleeve. It is easier to work with white or ivory based shirt backgrounds, but other colors will work. Just make sure your color choices work well for mix-and-match. Don't force colors together. A couple of examples: white ground with green/yellow/melon and blue overlay (windowpane design); melon background with an olive and navy multigraph pattern.

Other fabrics include microfiber for short-sleeve polos, short-sleeve shirts and crew-neck styles. These fabrics can be warm if you buy pure microfiber. It is best to buy blends of cotton and microfiber so the fabric will breathe better. Please note some of the new microfiber and cotton fiber technology will whisk perspiration from the skin to the top of the shirt surface to keep the skin cool and dry.

Silk or silk and cotton are other fiber choices for shirts and polos. Keep in mind that silk by itself can be hot, and perspiration stains can be pronounced.

Fall/winter tops

Cut and sewn long-sleeve shirt

☐ Solid twill, poplin or pinpoint weave non-iron button front, long sleeve, collared (point, hidden or button down) and button cuff. Basic and jewel tone colors are excellent for mix-and-match. Basic choices include white, black, ivory, silver, navy, ink blue, ecru, burgundy, rust and olive. Jewel tones include rose, kelly green, slate blue and berry.

☐   Muted patterned non-iron poplin button front, long sleeve, collared (point, hidden or button down) and button cuff. Use easy background color choices for maximum mix-and-match. Besides white, also consider that light gray, blue, ecru and olive are good examples for shirt backgrounds that have a window pane, multigraph pattern and muted plaids. Multi-stripe backgrounds will include black, navy and charcoal. These are just a few of many colors and patterns available.

In fall and winter, as the weather gets colder, we have a tendency to wear more clothes. Be sure to add light layers to add warmth but not bulk. Some shirt fabrics like flannel and wool are useful for layering, but use thin fabrics to balance your fit and appearance.

Other good long-sleeve shirt fabrics include microfiber or a blend with cotton, Tencel or silk drape and do not cling. You can also find cotton pique long sleeve polos.

Knits

Knits are made in long- or short-sleeve polos (soft collar), crew and mock neck styles. All three styles are appropriate for dressing casually in business. A soft collar, long sleeve is appropriate for fall and winter. Short sleeves are optional for spring and summer. The best fabrics to pick are the following: silk, silk and wool (fine-gauge) and cotton and rayon (gives a soft smooth feel, drapes and does not cling, a favorite for many people). Knits can be found as solids, mélange or marled weaves. The mélange or marled weaves are the twisting of two or more different thread colors to give the appearance of a fancy solid weave. Having multiple colors enables further mix-and-match with other pieces in your wardrobe.

☐   Solid polo (with soft collar, three-button placket), long sleeve (raglan for a smooth shoulder fit and comfort), knitted cuff and sleeve, made of 60/40 cotton/viscose (rayon). Good color choices include black, ivory, taupe, navy, charcoal, cocoa, olive, merlot, mustard and dark teal.

☐   Melange or marled long sleeve polo, cotton/viscose in a black/ivory, black/taupe or black/mustard. There are many color combinations.

☐ Mock or crew, solid, flat or ribbed weave, microfiber, long sleeve and open bottom. Medium to dark jewel tone colors give good contrast as a mix-and-match item. The following are colors to seek: black, ivory, sun (bright yellow), brick, berry, eggplant, turquoise and ink blue.

For casual dress, knits are an excellent choice. They fit well and stand on their own without a blazer or sport coat.

Sweaters

When jackets are not required, sweaters are a good option especially when it is cold out. Sweaters can be worn over a knit as layering pieces. The best styles are made as flat, cable or ribbed weaves in superfine cottons, worsted superfine wool yarns, silk and wool and silk and cotton fabrics. Pullover styles are predominant. There are zipper and button front cardigan sweater jacket designs that are outstanding for casual wear.

Buy any sweater in a good quality fabric that fits well and comes in colors that are suitable for mix-and-match with shirts, knits and slacks. Get a sweater that complements you and makes you look balanced and symmetrical. You don't want to add bulk or have a sloppy appearance.

☐ Black, ivory, taupe, olive, navy or charcoal, zip or button front longer cardigan or sweater jacket style, ribbed or cable weave, superfine cotton or wool. Silk and cotton or silk and wool are other good combination options.

☐ Solid black, ivory, red, berry, eggplant, green, olive, taupe, navy, charcoal, ink blue, and teal made in the following fabrics are excellent pullover sweaters: superfine cotton, wool and silk or silk and cotton, crew or V-neck, flat or ribbed knit with long sleeves.

☐ V-neck or crew-neck pullover woven in a mélange or marled flat or textured weave, superfine wool or cotton. Silk is an option. Blends of wool/silk/cotton, wool and silk, cotton and silk or other combinations including microfiber are all good fabrics that make a balanced fit.

When a jacket isn't required, choose fabrics that hold their shape, drape well and look fresh during the workday.

Slacks

Your slacks are just as important as your shirt, knit or sweater. Casual wear is dressing up, not down. When dressing casual, your slack selection is critical. Good fabric, the right model and proper fit sends the message that you are professional and serious about what you do even though a jacket isn't required.

It is important to select fabrics that have the latest technology: stretch, Teflon or stain resistant and wrinkle-resistant. High performance fabrics are available in wool, microfiber and non-iron cotton. Wool fabrics are available in worsted, gabardine, bedford cord, high twist, faille, serge and covert twill weaves. These materials have texture, which is ideal for mix-and-match.

Slacks fit high enough on the waist so hip bones are not defined or any underwear is exposed. You're not making a fashion statement or your own. Slacks should be neat, clean and pressed and of colors and fabrics that look professional. Save low riders and wild prints for the club or the beach on your own time.

Whether you select wool, cotton or microfiber, the fabrics should have good body, drape and make your body look symmetrical. Make sure when you fit your slacks that they come up high enough. You are not in jeans. The fit is totally different. See how to fit slacks in chapter 14.

Non-iron cotton slacks are available. The fabric is treated similar to the non-iron shirts. Good quality cotton is processed during the fabric manufacturing with non-iron technology. The fabric is pack-n-go; you simply wash, dry and wear. Wash with a mild detergent, cold water wash and place immediately in dryer for about 20 minutes, hang up and the slacks are ready to wear.

□ Solid black, taupe, olive, charcoal, oxford gray (mid-shade), medium or dark olive, British tan, khaki, navy and cocoa, superfine wool, stretch, strain and wrinkle-resistant, pleated or flat front

- Solid black, khaki, tan, taupe, olive, navy, cocoa or charcoal 100% microfiber (polyester) or polyester and viscose (rayon) blend. Select a twill or gabardine weave, pleated or flat front.

- Solid black, navy, tan, stone or chino, twill or gabardine weave, non-iron cotton slacks in a pleated or flat front

A note about jeans: Some firms allow jeans. If that is the case for you, select stretch denim. There are high-quality, better end jeans that give outstanding fit and good appearance. Regardless of the fabric, the fit and professional appearance is what is important.

Belts

Most belts used for business casual work with casual dress as well. Although the dress is not as formal, the message you send is no less professional. Belts and braces are used for business casual to casual dress.

Your leather belt should complement your shoes and be the same color. Just as with professional dress and business casual, never mix colors. Purchase belts made of Kip, calf-skin or waxhide leathers with a matte finish. Choose a solid strap or embossed belt that is 1 to 1 ⅛ inches in width, with a silver, gold, brass or silver and gold square or round buckle (keep metal color similar to your jewelry).

Belts to wear with jeans

Black or mid-tan waxhide or Nubuc leather, 1 ¼ to 1 ½ inches wide, square or round, silver, brass or dull finished gold buckle. Black/brown, tan/brown, black/tan braided, raised or combination weave, square or round, silver, brass or dull finished gold buckle. Match your belt color to your shoes.

Braces

If your slacks will not stay up with a belt, then use braces instead of a belt. Braces that have button tabs is the way to go. Do not buy suspenders that have metal clips that fasten on top of the waist band. There are many types of materials used for braces, but the best is leather. Braces are also available in elastic, rayon and silk, but these types of braces can quickly fray, curl and become limp in a short period of time. Braces made out of calf-skin, Kip or waxhide leather will last for a long time.

Leather braces come in solid straps, woven braids or textured styles. Black, burgundy or mid-tan shades are good colors. Match your braces to your shoes, and do not wear a belt when wearing braces.

- ☐ Kip, calf-skin or waxhide tan or brown solid strap, braid or embossed brace 1 to 1 ¼ inches wide, round or square, brass, gold, or silver keepers (buckles)

- ☐ Black solid strap, braid or embossed strap brace 1 inch wide, round square, brass, gold or silver keepers

Hosiery

Socks used for business casual can be used for casual dress. The differences are subtle – the fabric may be thicker or of a fine-gauge wool or cotton, flat or ribbed weave and may make more use of muted patterns than solids.

Your socks need to complement your outfit, not take away from it or be noticed. Make sure the length is long enough to cover your legs when you sit down and not expose any skin. Make sure whatever you pick looks professional and has a high-quality feel and fit so they do not sag or fall down.

Socks can be similar colors and shades to the slacks of the garment you plan to wear, but you do not have to match. Solids or small patterns are acceptable. Patterned socks add to the overall creativity of your garment as an added touch.

Fine-gauge cotton lisle or Merino wool in ribbed or flat weaves is good to pick. When choosing, it is best to make sure you are getting a good blend, 75/25, 65/35 or 80/20 in Merino/nylon or mercerized cotton lisle/nylon. This blend maintains the shape and helps keep shrinkage to a minimum. Choose quality socks. They'll stay up and not slide down.

Choose slack length or over-the-calf Merino wool or cotton lisle socks in black, navy, charcoal, olive, taupe, medium or dark brown, oxford or medium gray, tan, charcoal blue all in solid or pattern.

Shoes

With casual dress, you have a choice of shoe styles. Tie shoes in plain or cap toe or loafers in plain, kiltie/tassel or waxhide woven are all appropriate styles. See leather in chapter 7.

When going through a casual interview, your shoes can be a tie or slip-on style shoe. The best casual shoes are solid or embossed leathers in black, mid-tan, brown black/tan, black/brown and tan/tan combinations.

For comfort the best tie shoe styles are the open toe blucher as opposed to a bal oxford. The bal is closed at the point of lacing and can become tight when the shoes are tied. It is best to get shoes that have open toe blucher styles. The open toe blucher is woven open on the top vamp at the point where lacing of the shoe begins. This allows enough room when tying the shoes so they don't become tight across the top of your foot.

Shoes to wear with jeans

Waxhide and Nubuc leathers are excellent with jeans. You have a choice of tie or loafer styles. Tan, brown or black are the best shoe colors for jeans. With jeans wear a belt only, not braces. Match your belt colors to your shoes. Never mix colors, and keep the leather texture similar.

- ☐ Black, brown or tan waxhide or Nubuc tie shoe in a plain or cap toe (keep the texture smooth, not embossed)
- ☐ Black, brown or tan waxhide or Nubuc loafer in a penny strap, kiltie, kiltie tassel or plain toe style (choose solid or textured leather)

Outerwear

Business casual outerwear in most cases will work for casual wear. Outerwear you select should complement your casual wardrobe just as it would for business or professional dress. This is not the appropriate time or place to wear your favorite old leather jacket or your old college letter jacket.

You have a choice of wearing a microfiber all-weather coat. You also have a choice of wearing a good quality fingertip length such as a leather, shearling, wool or microfiber jacket. These jackets work well whether you are wearing a shirt, knit or sweater. If you wear a longer sweater, make sure your outerwear is long enough to cover the bottom of your knit or sweater entirely.

Remember, outerwear is the first, and sometimes the only, article of clothing seen and could set the tone for your image all by itself.

TIP
Never let your jacket on top stick out below your outerwear.

Fingertip-length jackets

☐ Solid black, charcoal or black olive Merino wool single-breasted, zip or button front and with a fill or removable liner. Additional color choices include taupe, tan or cocoa in solid, mélange, birdseye or herringbone weaves.

☐ Black plongé, lambskin leather or shearling, button front, permanent (for winter wear only), removable liner (for fall, winter and early spring wear). Brown and mid-tan are other colors you can consider.

☐ Black or charcoal, cotton or microfiber shell, removable liner, zip or button front

If you choose to wear jeans, leather, microfiber, shearling and wool jackets are the fabrics of choice. Any of these styles will look good with jeans.

13

No Jacket: Casual Dress for Women

Thank you to Dick and Shelly Lerner for helping me look my best in a casual environment. It's way harder than dressing in a perfectly pressed uniform – it's so easy to get casual wrong. I appreciate your knowledge of the fabrics and construction; it really does make all the difference in how I look.

– Sincerely, Caroline W.

Simply put, casual dress for women still needs to look professional. What you wear is not about the latest fashion style or trend – here one season, gone the next. It is about classic styling, but your look does not have to be stodgy, dowdy or flamboyant.

Defining casual business wear is difficult for women. There are so many mixed messages sent out by the women's clothing makers, women's magazines and star-studded TV images. For you, casual dress is about being able to go to your closet to pull out a top and slack that stand together as an outfit and will mix-and-match with other items in your wardrobe. It's about being able to wear what you have day in and day out throughout the year.

Fabrics need to fit and drape properly and hold their shape through the workday. When a jacket is not required, you rely on having good fabrics, proper fit and pulling your outfit together. Without a jacket, everything shows.

With casual dress, you can make yourself looked balanced and symmetrical with your choice of fabrics. When carefully paired, your clothing will not create distractions or be a barrier to your professional image.

Make sure your blouse, knit or sweater fits long enough to cover your slacks waistband and does not ride up. Never have your abdomen exposed. Your slacks need to fit high enough to cover skin and undergarments and not to expose or define curves.

Slacks

Select high performance wools, microfibers, cottons and triple stretch nylon/rayon/lycra fabrics that are stain and wrinkle-resistant. Make sure they fit properly with pleated or flat front. If you do choose a flat front, make sure it fits like a pleat especially when you sit down. You need plenty of room so your slacks won't wrinkle across the lap.

- ☐ Solid black, taupe, tan, eggplant, charcoal, olive, red and navy, flat front or pleated, side elastic or no waistband. Choose either a high performance wool or micro-fiber fabric.
- ☐ Solid triple stretch black, tan, taupe, navy, olive, chino or stone, flat front
- ☐ Solid wrinkle free cotton in black, chino, stone, olive, taupe or tan, flat front or pleated

Jeans

Jeans are acceptable for some companies, and if that is the case for you, make sure you select a better quality of jeans made from stretch denim. Your jeans need to send the same professional message as your slacks. Your fit can be no different than slacks. Jeans cannot be tight. The fit needs to drape and complement the top you pair with it. Select black, dark blue or stone blue, flat front stretch denim

Blouse/shell

Whatever top you choose, it should have a professional look, fit well, should not define shapes and curves and be long enough to cover your abdomen.

You have choices to wear: blouses or shells. Blouses can be solids, patterns or stripes. It's not just white; you can pick blue, ink blue, rose, ecru, yellow, apple green, taupe, khaki, olive, pink, black, silver or burgundy for solid colors. These are just a few of many examples.

Where available, choose non-iron cotton pinpoint oxford or poplin cotton fabrics for easy care. These blouses maintain their shape all day long. Choices of collar styles include button down, point, closed and spread colors.

Button cuff styles are good for casual wear. Convertible cuffs are available, like a button cuff. There is an extra cut by the button that allows you to wear cuff links.

If you choose a stripe or pattern blouse, try to pick white ground backgrounds. They will be easier to mix-and-match with other wardrobe items. You can choose small, medium or wide stripes or multi-stripe blouses. Patterns can be a small multicolored window pane, plaid or graph check.

Shells make a good alternative to a blouse. The best styles are jewel or crew-neck that sits at the base of the neck. Solids are easier to work with. Patterns can be more difficult to mix-and-match. When selecting pattern shells, make sure the colors will work with multiple items.

Blouses

- □ Solid non-iron cotton or microfiber blue, pink, ecru, taupe, khaki, deep blue (ink), rose, silver, charcoal, melon, apple green and gold. Long sleeve, button cuffs and point collar styles are the most versatile models. These styles are easy to mix-and-match with other components of your wardrobe.

☐ White ground pin or tape stripe, blue, red, charcoal, navy, green or rose. Long sleeve, button cuffs and point collar styles; excellent for mix-and-match with other components of your wardrobe. Try to get non-iron cotton fabrics, so your blouse looks fresh all day long.

☐ Pattern white ground graph check or window pane pattern long sleeve, button cuff blouses. More colors in the blouse will allow more mix-and-match capabilities.

Shells

☐ Solid shells in long-sleeve, flat weave, crew or jewel neck in ivory, black, navy, red, taupe, pink, eggplant, ink blue and olive, among many colors available. Microfiber or stretch cotton (cotton and lycra in a flat or ribbed weave) are outstanding choices and are easy care, pack-n-go and hold their shape all day long and do not cling. Short sleeve (spring/summer) styles are best worn under a blazer or sport jacket. Of the fabrics available microfiber would be the primary choice and then stretch cotton.

Knits

Knits made of fine-gauge wool, silk, silk/wool, acrylic, acrylic/cotton and stretch cotton (blend of cotton and lycra) have a professional look and drape well to the body, and keep their shape. They are excellent for mix-and-match.

Solid colors such as ivory, black, charcoal, taupe, red, mocha and eggplant are excellent for mix-and-match with slacks. There are fancy nondescript patterns called mélanges that mix two or three yarns together: black and ivory, black and taupe, mocha and tan are just some of many examples.

Preferred models are high V-neck, jewel, crew or mock neck, long sleeve, three-quarter sleeve length, knitted cuff and bottom or open sleeve and bottom. These garments stand on their own and work well underneath a jacket or sweater.

☐ Solid ivory, black, charcoal, taupe, red, mocha, eggplant, olive, soft yellow, rose, pink, slate blue and navy three-quarter or long sleeve mock, jewel, high V-neck or crew-neck. Consider having more than one of these popular knits that are good for mix-and-match.

☐ Nondescript/marled or mélange pattern in an ivory/black, tan/black, gray/black, brick/tan, olive/tan, blue/black, burgundy/black and burgundy/tan. These are just a few of the many combinations available. Mock, jewel, high V-neck or crew-neck style knits are available in a flat knit weave.

Sweaters

Sweaters should never fit tight or show shapes or curves. You want to be as professional in appearance as if you were wearing a jacket. Longer cardigan styles (upper-thigh length that covers the seat), zip or button fronts will work in place of a jacket. Choose sweaters of solid ribbed or flat weaves made of silk, wool, silk/wool blends or fine-gauge cotton. Cashmere and camel hair are luxury fibers that will not hold up to rigorous wear. Keep these for special occasions. Merino wool in a fine-gauge weave is outstanding quality; it holds its shape and lasts. Purchase garments that feel luxurious and have high quality as they are more likely to last.

Blouses, shells or knits can all be worn underneath a sweater with either a skirt or slacks. If you select pullover sweater styles, make sure they fit and do not cling. You never want to show a tight fit that promotes too much shape or curve; it is not a professional look. The best collar styles are high V-neck, crew or boat necks in a flat or ribbed weave. Look for the same fabric content mentioned for the longer cardigan sweaters.

Solid long cardigan, button or zip front, ribbed or flat weave, cotton, wool or silk and wool. The following colors are excellent: black, navy, ivory, taupe, tan, olive, soft yellow, rose, pink and chocolate. Solid long sleeve or three quarter sleeve, high V-neck, crew or boat neck, cotton, silk and wool or Merino wool, ribbed or flat weave in black, ivory, taupe, tan, navy, salmon, soft yellow, rose, pink, olive, navy or slate blue

Belts

Belts are optional. If you choose to wear one, it should highlight your casual wear items and help complete your outfit. Belts should always match the color of your shoes and purse. Never mix colors.

You have the choice of wearing solid straps or embossed leathers that look like exotic skins. Buy well-made leather belts such as calf-skin or Kip leathers. These leathers hold their shape and finish and can be refinished after extensive wear. Good leather lasts a long time. With proper care, belts will remain an integral part of your wardrobe.

Transition from business casual to casual with belts that are ¾ to 1 ½ inches wide, round or square, brass, gold, silver or a combination of gold and silver, round or square buckle style in these colors and textures:

- ☐ Solid or embossed strap in black, burgundy, brown, mid-tan
- ☐ Other good colors are red, navy, taupe, winter white and raisin

Hosiery

When you wear casual slacks, either panty hose or socks can be worn. You can pick solid or small pattern styles and match a color similar to the slacks. Length should be high enough not to expose your skin when sitting. Choose hosiery in the following colors: solid or nondescript pattern in black, charcoal, navy, taupe, tan or olive.

Shoes

Casual shoes need to look professional too. Don't be tempted to follow the latest fashion trend. Shoes also need to be comfortable and fit properly. Even with casual dress, open-toed shoes and sandals and bare legs are not professional in the workplace.

Pumps that are calf-skin, aniline leather or Nubuc, solid or embossed, plain toe, cap toe or with a woven surface and heel height of 1 to 1 ½ inches, with a combination leather and vibram or rubber sole are excellent styles to wear. These shoes can be worn with either skirts or slacks.

Loafers that are flat and without ribbons or metal decoration, plain or cap toe, are good styles for your business casual wardrobe. Aniline or calf-skin solid or embossed, waxhide leather (natural or oil skin finish) are good picks. These types of leathers have no limits to what you can coordinate with them.

Tie shoes look great with casual slacks. Calf-skin, aniline leather, waxhide, Nubuc, solid skin, plain or cap toe, vibram and leather combinations or rubber soles are good selections to make. Choose a good pair of tie shoes when you are dressing casually at work and you will be on your feet during the day.

Black, burgundy and mid-tan are good colors to start with. Once you have your basics, you can add taupe, navy, red and chocolate. These colors will help round out your wardrobe. All these colors look professional and are good for mix-and-match.

Pumps

Black pumps with a combination or rubber sole, heel height 1 to 1 ½ inches, calf-skin, aniline or Nubuc leather. The aniline or calf-skin leather can be solid or embossed. Have at least two pairs of black shoes, even three pair, so you can rotate during the week. This will help keep your shoes wearing longer without wearing out.

- Burgundy, mid-tan, taupe, navy and red with a combination or rubber sole, heel height 1 to 1 ½ inches, calf-skin or aniline leather, solid or embossed
- Chocolate Nubuc, heel height 1 to 1 ½ inches with a combination or rubber sole

Flats/loafers

Black, plain or cap toe, solid or embossed leather, no ribbons or metal decoration, flat, combination or rubber sole. Get at least two pair or more, so you can rotate through the week. This way, you won't wear your shoes out quickly. Choose calf-skin, aniline, waxhide or Nubuc leather.

☐ Mid-tan, burgundy, navy, taupe and red, solid or embossed leather, combination or rubber sole and flat not thick soles

☐ Chocolate Nubuc, combination or rubber sole, plain toe flat

Tie shoes

☐ Black plain or cap toe, combination or vibram sole

☐ Mid-tan, burgundy or brown, plain or cap toe, combination or vibram sole

☐ Black, brown or tan Nubuc or waxhide plain toe, combination or vibram sole

Outerwear

Long coats can be used for professional, business casual and casual wear. Long coats, fingertip and pant coat lengths are all good styles to pick from – it is a matter of personal preference. A shorter style coat length is usually mid-thigh or just above the knee.

Microfiber, cotton, wool, shearling, leather and micro-suede are all good choices for casual wear. These fabrics are professional, durable and enhance your casual look.

If your budget allows, cashmere, camel hair, mohair and angora can be considered, but be careful not to wear these in wet winter weather Wear these luxury fibers only when it is cold and dry outside.

☐ Cotton, twill, gabardine or peachface (see term on page 92), fingertip length, zip or button front and removable liner. Black and tan are primary colors to consider; other colors can include olive, mocha, navy, taupe, stone and cement.

☐ Microfiber, fingertip or pant coat (just above or below the knee), button front, removable liner. Primary colors are black, charcoal, taupe, tan and stone. You can consider eggplant, olive, rose and steel blue as alternative colors. These shades should be deep tones to give good contrast with your casual apparel.

☐ Merino or lamb's wool, solid, mélange, birdseye or herringbone weave, fingertip or pant coat length, removable liner if available and button front. Black, charcoal, olive, taupe, tan, navy and red are excellent choices of color; black and white, black and gray, black and olive, black and tan, black and taupe and taupe and oatmeal are all excellent color choices for mélange, birdseye and herringbone weaves.

☐ Micro suede solid, fingertip or pant coat length, button front and removable liner if available. Black, tan and taupe are excellent colors. Slate, rose, cement and forest green are alternative colors.

☐ Leather or shearling, fingertip, pant coat or full length, shearling lining and leather removable liner (transition leather coat wear for the different seasons) and button or zip front. If you choose leather, choose a good lamb or calf-skin; make sure leathers are thick enough to last, yet supple to your touch. Stay away from leather that is stiff or thin. A good leather will last for years.

14

Does This Fit?

*A*fter 20 years in the military, I'd forgotten how *to dress – that is until the Lerners taught me about fabric and proper fit. They have shown me the value of building a great wardrobe. Now my wardrobe makes sense and will last for a long time.*

– Ron Belyan

Now that you know which garments you need to build your wardrobe, it's time to purchase your apparel. At some point, you will find yourself standing in front of a mirror and wondering, "Does this fit?"

The Big Fish knows. The purpose of this chapter is to help you understand how clothes are supposed to fit and what to do to ensure the proper fit. You won't feel like a fish out of water once you are armed with the right information.

Fit means fitting in the sense of its appropriateness for your overall business wardrobe, but for the purposes of this chapter, fit means "this garment fits your body." Size, length, width, too tight, too loose? Once again, your image defines you, and the clothing you choose becomes your signature. But having the perfect pieces only works if they fit you perfectly.

TIP

You never want to look as if you haven't come to terms with how you look. Properly fitting clothes will help you carry yourself with pride and confidence.

Men and women hurt themselves by not checking to see if their clothing fits right. Rarely does clothing fit perfectly at first; most often, it needs to be altered. Don't just take clothing off the rack and start wearing it. If something needs to be altered, it is best to use a professional tailor who is familiar with proper fitting techniques.

If the clothes you wear during an interview hang on you or are too tight or too long, your interviewer will notice. Good "fit" is your opportunity to "sweat the small details" and show the interviewer or your employer that you are productive and consistent. Getting hired or advancing in your career or conducting business can sometimes come down to dress and appearance – who looks the part.

We all have different shapes, sizes and to get the right fit will be uniquely your own. Your head may sit erect or lean forward (head forward position). You may stand erect or slouch forward. Your shoulders may sit square, regular or slope – perfectly normal.

Give yourself a test. Check your body to see how it can and will affect the fit of your jacket. Take your fingers and go to the top of your shoulders at about the middle, you may have your clavicle protruding upward, again, perfectly normal.

Now take your fingers to the base of your neck, both sides, where you may feel on one or both sides that it feels hollow – this is normal.

Next, go to where your upper arm joins your chest. Find the edge of your shoulder. It may feel as if it is rounding forward – it probably is.

Take your fingers down to your side, at the hip bones, go back about 2 inches on your back waist. You will feel extra skin sitting there, also normal.

The reason you did this is to show you as we all get older, our body starts changing. Stay aware of your body and watch for changes as you get older – most people notice changes starting in their 20s and then throughout their life. This is why you need to know where your body is now and what you have to do to get the right fit.

Know your body. Understand what difficulties you have getting your clothing to look as you want to be seen. The challenge is to get your body and your clothing to fit as one – balanced and symmetrical.

Your Mirror Image

Your suit coat, sport coat or blazer is about 90 percent of your visual. It makes a huge impact. Your jacket needs to complement your body, not detract from it. Here's how to get a good fit, accept no less. Always be fit in front of a three-way mirror so you can see yourself from the front, side and back. Take special note of these items:

Collar: Make sure it fits snugly around your neck, no gaps. If it sits off your neck, a tailor can "shrink it down" using a heavy thread to lock it down on one side, weaving it through the collar so it goes around the neck and then locking it down on the other side.

This alteration will not be seen because it is done along the inside. Normally this will take care of any gaping. More severe gaping may require the collar to be shortened. In either case, the collar has to fit snugly around your neck.

If you are wearing a shirt or blouse, the collar should be about 1 inch above the jacket collar. Use this as a guide. If it is within a quarter inch, you will be fine.

Neck/shoulders/bicep: Around the base of the neck can be hollow on one or both sides. If this occurs when you put your jacket on, the easiest way to fix this is have your tailor lightly pad to fill in the space; this will make it smooth.

Look at the back of your neck and make sure there is no roll underneath your collar. If there is, it means your coat is too long for your body. This can be corrected by having your tailor raise the material from the center point of shoulders from nothing and gradually increase the amount necessary to get rid of the roll and gradually reducing down to nothing at the opposite shoulder center point. This alteration is often referred to as "lower the collar" or "raise the back". Do not overlook this alteration – it makes a big difference!

The shoulder line of your jacket needs to be smooth. If it is not, have your tailor lightly pad under the shoulder affected; it could be both. If you have a hollow area between your body and fit of the jacket, this normally takes care of the problem.

Look at your biceps on both arms, at the point where the shoulder line and sleeves join it extends far enough out not to cause a divot above your bicep. If this happens, it means the point-to-point of the jacket is too narrow for your body. Your jacket shoulder line needs to be wider to get away from this problem. As you get older, your upper biceps get thicker, and you need to have enough room in your sleeves so you are comfortable and the "sleeve head" lies flat. Upper sleeve material should not dip inward.

Shoulder blades/center seam: Look at the back of your shoulder blades in the mirror. Make sure there is no excess fabric, on one or both sides. If there is, your tailor will need to use padding to fill in the hollow areas; the appearance needs to be smooth. A little extra fabric is fine on the back shoulders, so when you extend your arms forward you are not so tight you rip the material in the back of the coat.

If your shoulder blades are pronounced, this can cause excess material to collect at the center seam of your jacket. This is corrected by your tailor opening the back collar and center seam and taking in the excess amount far enough down your back until the material feels comfortable and smooth.

Chest/lapels/coat front and back waist: The chest of your jacket should lie flat and be comfortable. Both sides of the jacket come almost to the center of your sternum. Make sure you have no folds to the side of your chest. If you do, have your tailor lightly pad the area affected; this normally will fix it.

Make sure your lapels lie flat. If they pouch out, you will need to have your tailor shrink them down. Barrel chests or the length of lapels cause this to happen. Shrinking the lapels is similar to the collar tailoring. All it takes is to gather the material inside the lapel by weaving a thread, gathering the fabric and locking the material in place. This cannot be seen and gets rid of the bulge; more extreme cases may require shortening the lapel straps.

Your coat waist, front and back, needs to fit comfortably and accommodate whatever you carry on the inside pockets, such as a cell phone, wallet, PDA and other items. When your coat is buttoned, make sure you have about ¾ inch extra room between your abdomen and coat so it is not pulling, with no horizontal lines at the waist or pulling at the back. If your coat is vented, make sure the vent is closed, not open.

A quick test to make sure you have a good fit at your coat waist: Unbutton your coat. Each side should be about 1 inch apart, when opened.

The fit corrections that have been detailed are often overlooked. Make sure when you are getting fit or having alterations done to look in the mirror and make sure everything is fitting smoothly and is balanced and symmetrical. Ultimately, your clothing makes a powerful statement about you.

Slack/skirt waistbands: If you have a problem with your waistband rolling when you are standing or sitting, have your tailor put stiffening web material inside the waistband.

Get Fit Checklist

Here are examples that will help you fine tune your fit.

MEN

Jacket

- ☐ Fit your collar snug so it does not gap around your neck.
- ☐ Make sure there is no extra fabric gathered under the back of the collar.
- ☐ Your jacket should not be wrinkled across the shoulder blades.

☐ Make sure the coat waist is comfortable in front and back. If your coat has a vent, make sure it is closed. If your coat has no vent, make sure it lies flat on your back waist and hips, not pulling.

☐ The length should come to upper-thigh on the side and cover your seat.

☐ Sleeves should be fit at the break of the wrist.

☐ Shoulder line should be smooth, not broken, with no puckers or gaps. If not, light top padding will need to be added.

☐ Your jacket is 90 percent of your visual image. Make sure there is nothing to cause distractions or detract from your message.

Slacks

☐ Fit your waist comfortably without being snug. Make sure the waistband is stiff so it will not roll over when you stand or sit.

☐ If you buy a pleated model, this allows your abdomen to expand without causing wrinkling across the lap. The pleats should face out to the pockets not toward the zipper; this model has a more slenderizing fit.

☐ If you buy a flat front model, make sure it fits as full as a pleated model. Otherwise your slacks will be so tight they will wrinkle across the lap. If the material is stressed over a period of time, it will become weak and split.

☐ If your pants are baggy or the crotch droops, take in excess material from the outside seam. The crotch can be shortened up to ½ inch. Any more and the fit will not be symmetrical. If you can't keep your pants up on your waist with a belt, wear braces.

☐ Length should come to the top of the heel with a slight break in front. Cuff the bottoms. Cuff size can be 1¼ inches.

Shirts/soft tops

- ☐ Fit the chest, waist and hips comfortably, with no pulling.
- ☐ Collar point length 3 inches. Back collar width 1 ¾ inches wide to cover your tie; your tie cannot show underneath.
- ☐ Neck large enough to allow for shrinkage. A good test is if you can get one or two fingers in your collar buttoned.
- ☐ Make sure the tail length comes down 4 to 6 inches inside the waistband. If not, the tail of the garment won't stay in.
- ☐ If you have a long sleeve, make sure the length comes to the break of the wrist; otherwise, the sleeves will be short.
- ☐ Make sure the cuff is large enough to glide over your watch and wrist without restriction.

Tie

- ☐ Defines your creativity. It binds your outfit together.
- ☐ Length needs to come to the top, middle or bottom of waistband. Make sure there are no waves or puckers in the front of the tie and that it is lined end-to-end and edge-to-edge. There should be at least two or three layers of inside lining (cotton, wool or muslin) to give the tie body.
- ☐ Length should be no less than 54 inches. For a man with a height of 5 feet 8 inches to 6 feet, the ideal tie length is 56 to 58 inches. For men from 6 feet 1 inch to 6 feet 3 inches tall, ties should be 59 to 61 inches long. A man 6 feet 3 inches and taller should wear a tie length of 63 to 66 inches. There should never be any part of the shirt exposed from the bottom of the tie to the waistband of the pant.
- ☐ Select a pure silk in a solid, micro-screen, tone-on-tone jacquard, panel, parque, vertical or horizontal stack, geometric or nondescript multi-patterns. Popular colors include eggplant, burgundy, taupe and navy, black, olive, yellow, red, tan, silver, gray and charcoal.

Shoes

- ☐ Shoes are one of the most important articles you wear. Your shoes say a lot about you!

- ☐ Don't ruin the image you project with shoes that are worn out or are the wrong style.

- ☐ For dress, the best tie shoe styles are plain, cap toe, split toe panel or wing-tips; loafers can be worn for professional, business casual and casual, not for the formal interview.

- ☐ The best leather for shoes is either calf-skin or aniline. These skins have a duller finish and are thicker. These leathers do not peel easily and hold the finish.

- ☐ Make sure your shoes are in good shape.

- ☐ Check and make sure your heels are not worn down. If so, replace the heels by a shoemaker. Shoe care and appearance is so important for your outfit, and shoe maintenance is a very important part. Nothing is worse than having shoes with worn away heels.

- ☐ Make sure the soles have no holes and that the shoe edge has a good finish.

- ☐ Most important, make sure your shoes have a good shine. If you can't get a good shine, take them to a shoe repair shop and let them either refinish or give your shoes a good polish.

Hosiery

Never go to formal events, meetings or interviews with short socks – never expose your legs or leg hair. For formal interviews, sock colors can be solid or a muted pattern in black, navy, charcoal or oxford gray in a wool or cotton/nylon blend – weave can be a flat or ribbed weave.

- ☐ Keep sock colors similar to your pants – doesn't have to match. Pattern socks do not have to match the tie; keep the colors similar. Sock patterns show your creativity.

- [ ] For professional dress, black, navy and charcoal are the predominant colors followed by taupe, tan, brown and olive; the same colors can be used for business casual dress.

Belt/braces/briefcases/folios

If you choose to wear a belt or braces, make sure you match the color to your shoes; black-to-black, burgundy-to-burgundy and brown-to-brown – never mix black-to-brown or burgundy-to-brown, and so on.

Briefcases or folios are something you carry – it is not worn. Colors do not have to match your belt or shoes. Brown, black, oak (tan) or burgundy are good colors to choose from. Can be made of leather, microfiber, or canvas.

WOMEN

Jacket

- [ ] Make sure there is no extra fabric gathered under the back of the collar.
- [ ] Your jacket should not be wrinkled across the shoulder blades.
- [ ] Make sure the coat waist is fit comfortably in front and back.
- [ ] The length should come to the upper-thigh on the side and cover the seat in back.
- [ ] Sleeves should be fit at the break of the wrist.
- [ ] Your jacket shoulder line should be smooth, not broken, puckered or show any gaps. If not, light top padding will need to be added.
- [ ] Your jacket is 90 percent of your visual image. Make sure there is nothing to cause distractions or detract from your message.

Skirt

- ☐ Fit your waist and abdomen comfortably without being snug; make sure waistband is stiff so it will not roll over when standing or sitting. Buy skirts that feature an elastic waistband and darts or soft tucks – to keep your abdomen from wrinkling.

- ☐ The length of a mid-length skirt should be three fingers above to three fingers below the knee. Short skirts are inappropriate for the interview or office.

- ☐ The hem of a long skirt should come just to the top of the back of the calf.

Slacks

- ☐ Make sure your waistband is comfortable and stiff so it will not roll over when you stand or sit.

- ☐ Your pant should be pleated. This allows your abdomen to expand without causing wrinkling across the lap. The pleats should face out to the pockets not toward the zipper; this model has a more slenderizing fit.

- ☐ If you choose a flat or plain front pant model, make sure the fit is full like a pleat. Plain or flat front pants often do not allow enough room for the abdomen to expand and can wrinkle across the lap.

- ☐ If your pants are baggy or the crotch droops, take in excess material from the outside seam. The crotch can be shortened up to ½ inch. Any more the fit will not be symmetrical.

- ☐ Your length should come to the top of the heel and a slight break in front. On pleated pants, cuff the bottoms. Cuff size can be 1 or 1 ⅛ inches. Flat front models normally are not cuffed.

Blouses/shells

- ☐ Make sure the fit is comfortable around your neck so there is enough room and will allow for shrinkage.

- ☐ Fit so the chest, bust, waist and hips are comfortable and there is no pulling, but do not fit tight and do not pronounce or define shapes and curves.

- ☐ Make sure the tail length comes down 4 to 6 inches inside the waistband. If not, the tail of the garment won't stay tucked in. No bare skin at front, side or back waist. You have to be completely covered.

- ☐ If you have a long sleeve, make sure the sleeve length comes to the break of the wrist; otherwise, the sleeves will be short.

- ☐ Make sure the cuff is large enough to glide over your watch and wrist without restriction.

Scarves

- ☐ A scarf shows your creativity. It binds your outfit together.

- ☐ Do not wear a chain or pearls with a scarf, it's too much around the neck. Pick one or the other.

- ☐ An oblong scarf is an easy style to work with. It is long and narrow and easy to tie in a variety of different knots.

- ☐ Select a pure silk in a solid, tone-on-tone jacquard or nondescript multi-pattern. Popular colors include eggplant, burgundy, taupe and navy.

Shoes

- ☐ Shoes are one of the most important articles you wear. Your shoes say a lot about you.

- ☐ Don't ruin the image you project with worn out or the wrong style shoes.

- ☐ Cheaply made shoes are cheap.

- ☐ The best shoe styles are either "V" or "U" shape pumps. Select plain or cap toe styles.

- ☐ The best leather for shoes is either calf-skin or aniline. These leathers do not peel easily and hold the finish. Heel height is 1 to 1 ½ inches.

- ☐ Make sure your shoes are in good shape.

- ☐ Check and make sure your heels aren't worn down. If you can, replace the heels.

- ☐ Make sure the soles have no holes and that the edges have a good finish.

- ☐ Most important, make sure your shoes have a good shine. If you can't get a good shine yourself, take them to a shoe repair shop and let them shine or refinish the shoes.

Hosiery

- ☐ Never go to formal events, meetings or interviews without hose. Wear neutral color hose so you don't draw attention to your outfit.

- ☐ When you wear a pantsuit, hose is an option. You can wear solid or small pattern socks. Color is a similar shade to your pant – but doesn't have to match.

Purse/belt/briefcases

- ☐ Your purse is something you wear. Match the color of your shoes to your purse. Do not mix colors.

- ☐ If you choose to wear a belt, make sure you match the color to your shoes and purse.

- ☐ Briefcases or folios are something you carry – it is not worn. Colors do not have to match your purse, belt or shoes. Brown, black, oak (tan) or burgundy are good colors to choose from. Can be made of leather, micro-fiber, or canvas.

15

The Difference Is In The Details

You really set me up with a great business wardrobe. From the first day of my new job as a management consultant with a top firm, I've been able to let my skills shine by always being impeccably dressed. Thank you!
– Wade Watts, Lieutenant Colonel (Ret.), ASAF

Jewelry, hats, gloves, beards, mustaches, eyeglasses, bracelets, perfume – the difference is truly in the details.

Personal hygiene and non-clothing items can be just as important to your image as how you put yourself together. Make it a habit to pay close attention to the appearance of your hair, use of hair care products, glasses, cosmetics, facial hair, fingernails, fragrances, cleanliness and jewelry. It shows you sweat the small details. How you take care of the small details impacts the overall picture you present – your image.

Personal appearance items need to be defined and practiced well before the interview, starting a job or anything important you are involved with. A careful and planned out image is powerful and captivating and shows you have done your homework. You are at the top of your game. Be effective in how you communicate and how you are seen.

Good grooming and personal hygiene are serious issues and not to be taken lightly.

Personal hygiene for men (and some tips for women too)

Facial hair: Men, inquire if a beard, mustache or goatee is acceptable for the interview. If you are told it is okay – fine. If you do not get a definite yes, go to the interview clean shaven. Facial hair should not be an obstacle or a distraction. There is enough to get through the interview process without having another item you cannot control. You certainly don't want to give advantage to another candidate competing for the same job. Facial hair should never impede trust.

Once you get the job, you may be able to grow the beard or mustache of your choice. Clear it first with your company.

There is nothing wrong with facial hair, but grooming it does become somewhat high maintenance. Beards, mustaches or goatees should be the same color as the hair on your head. No exceptions. Cleanliness, neatness and impeccable grooming are paramount. Be careful to avoid making yourself look older, disheveled or unkempt. If you want to be promoted, never let facial hair get in your way.

Make sure there is no hair or whiskers growing above or around your lip, sides of your mouth, cheeks or chin.

Renegade hair: Make sure you have no bushy neck or hair coming out of the nostrils or earlobes. Besides being well groomed, it shows you care about your appearance and pay attention to the small details. This says volumes about you as an individual – that you are task oriented and do not let small details get by you. It may not be important to you – but be assured it is to someone hiring you.

Hairstyle: It doesn't matter if you have a full head of hair, are almost bald, or bald – your hairstyle says a lot about you and your personality. If you only have several strands of hair, do not make it the focal point accentuated by using a gel to hold it in place. Your hairstyle needs to look and feel natural – fit the shape of your face and eyeglasses. Employ the services of a knowledgeable stylist who will work with you to help define a hairstyle that will work for interviewing, work and everything else.

Hair shouldn't be noticed but should be an underlying strength of your image. It should enhance not detract. If your face is full or thin, long or oval, or your ears are large or small – proper hairstyle brings the overall visual into balance.

Hair care products: The end result of a hair care product should make your hair look natural – not dry or oily. If a dandruff problem exists, get it under control. Work with a hair care professional to assess what products will eliminate or keep the dandruff down to a minimum.

Eyebrows: Too often overlooked. Eyebrows are not meant to be a bush. They can make you look older than you are. Keep eyebrows trimmed and neat. You never want to draw attention above your eyes. Women, don't make them too thin either, they frame your face.

Eyeglasses: Your eyes are your most important assets. They need to be seen not hidden. Lenses should be clear and cannot change color when you come in from the outdoors or vice versa. Work with an eyeglass professional to help you select eyeglasses that will work best for your facial shape and coloring.

Frames need to complement the shape of your face and your hairstyle. They should have color similar to tortoise shell. Monochromatic styles blend so much that there is no separation between skin tone and the glasses themselves. Color gives definition. It needs to be balanced and professional. Thickness of frames should enhance your appearance, not take away from it.

Jewelry: Two words: understated and classic. Jewelry should not be gaudy or overdone. Jewelry is something you wear, so it shouldn't be the center of attention. Its use is to accent your outfit, not to be the focal point. Wear no more than five or six items at a time. You don't want to wear too much where it detracts from your message.

- ☐ Wear one ring per hand. No more.

- ☐ Wear no more than six items of jewelry at one time.

- ☐ Keep the colors similar, gold, silver or a combination of both, in classic styles. Jewelry and accessories are to help finish off your outfit, not become the focal point of it.

- ☐ Your watch should be thin and round or a square shape with a white or gold face, sweep hand and a leather band. Metal watchbands eat cuff ends. If you ever wonder why the cuffs of your shirts fray, metal bands are infamous for this.

- ☐ Bracelets should be thin and understated not gaudy or heavy. When worn should not make any noise or be noticed.

- ☐ Lapel pins, if worn, should be small, not loud and be a complement to your outfit.

Fragrances: Too much is too much. Your fragrance should not be noticed from across the room. You never want to cause an allergic reaction especially during an interview, business meeting or working with a client. What you like may be offensive to someone else. The scent should not be noticed. Fragrances can be counterproductive with your body chemistry; it depends on the acid level that comes through your perspiration. Higher amounts can be noticed more with fragrances and deodorants – in fact, you may be noticed for the wrong reasons.

Deodorants: Should have no scent. Their job is to keep you dry and not yellow out the armholes of your shirts. High acid levels in perspiration with use of a scented deodorant can result in a more offensive odor. This is not what you intended.

Underarms: Like your hair and facial hair, underarm hair is high maintenance. It's important first to trim or shave your underarms. Do not allow dirt or bacteria to collect in the hair follicles. Keeping underarms shaved or trimmed short helps keep acid from transferring to the armpit of the shirt and to yellow and harden. Professionally, it's tough to find something more offensive than yellow stained armpits on your shirts.

Use a mild soap like Ivory or Dove – unscented. Soap that is scented used along with a scented deodorant along with high levels of acid in perspiration can lead to an offensive odor.

Cosmetics: Use concealers to hide any facial blemishes that may exist and to enhance an energized look. Use lightly to hide flaws and don't cake it on.

It is important to make your skin tone look as natural as you can without being over done. Skin tone varies from a yellow to a red tone – warm or cool. Yellow base skin looks sallow and washed out. Red base skin can look intimidating and overbearing. Properly used cosmetics help achieve a fresh, clean, well groomed look, enhancing your features.

Nails: Keep nails trimmed and manicured. There is no excuse for dirty fingernails, or nails not trimmed properly. This is a direct reflection of you. It shows how you pay attention to details. It is especially important to have your nails well manicured if you bite them.

Accessories for men

Cuff links: If you choose to wear cuff links, choose gold, silver or a combination of both. Keep the colors similar to your watch, ring, belt buckle and anything else you may wear. Pick classic styles – they can be cutting edge with or without a stone inlay; avoid cuff links that are too flashy. Cuff links are another item to help polish your outfit but should not become the focal point.

Umbrella: Choose either one that collapses or a long fixed style. Make sure the quality complements your outfit. A collapsible umbrella is good to have and keep in your briefcase if you get caught in an unexpected shower.

Briefcase/folio: Pick a classic style. You do not have to match colors to your belt, braces or shoes. Either item is something you carry, not wear. Choose from leather, canvas or microfiber in tan, brown, black or burgundy. Make sure it is not too large or bulky.

Hats: You have a choice of a cap or hat. Caps that have a good professional appearance are called cuffley caps. Their design is a solid piece of wool that has a brim bill in front. Black, charcoal, British tan or navy are good colors to pick but keep the color similar to your coat.

If you desire a hat instead, a brim that goes up in back and down in front or a full down turn style are good styles to pick. You have a choice of wool or felt, in a 2 or 3x width brim (approximately 2 to 3 inches in width). Solid black or charcoal are the best colors to pick from because so many top coats are black and gray. Other colors that are good are navy, tan, gray, taupe and brown, but keep your hat color similar to your coat.

When the weather gets cold, put on a hat. Not only does it look professional, it is healthy for you. If you are balding or have all your hair, covering up your head helps keep you warm.

Gloves: Cover up your hands with leather (lamb, glove, calf or aniline) dress gloves with a Thinsulate, cashmere, shearling or fur lining. It keeps your hands from getting frost bitten and looks professional with your winter or all-weather coat.

Scarves: Pick a lamb's wool, Merino, cashmere, camel hair or silk and wool scarf. Black, burgundy, charcoal or ivory are excellent solid colors to pick. These colors go well with most winter and all-weather coat colors. Pick a long, narrow, oblong style so it fits and rests well around your neck. Not only does it keep you warm, but it looks great. See page 134 for notes on cashmere and camel hair.

Personal hygiene for women (and some for men)

When going through the interview process, it is especially important you dress as best you can and can afford. The same should be true for your grooming and hygiene. A well-kept appearance is something to be maintained consistently.

Clothes should be always clean, pressed and in good shape. There should be no body odor whatsoever on your garments. If there is, do not wear them until they have been cleaned and pressed properly.

Hair: If hair length is longer than shoulder length, hair should be pulled up off the shoulder and secured with a conservative hairclip. Hair should never make a fashion statement. Never play with your hair in an interview or work situation. You never want to create a distraction that will take away from your ability to communicate.

Nail polish: For interviewing, office work or business meetings, polish should be clear or neutral, nothing bright that will draw attention or cause a distraction.

Lipstick: Clear or neutral or color that is a low gloss will not cause any distraction.

Mascara: If used, do so lightly. Eye makeup should only be used as a highlight.

Fragrances: Your perfume should have a slight scent but not strong. You do not want to cause an allergic reaction with the person you are meeting, especially during an interview.

Tattoos: If you tattoo any part of your body, make sure the tattoo can never be seen when you are dressed for work. Tattoos on legs, ankles, arms and back of the neck are almost impossible to hide. If you are interviewing, it's not an item you want seen or discussed. It's nothing that you would want to get in the way of being selected for the job, nor should it get in the way during client meetings or business meetings. Tattoos are often done on a whim that can have ramifications later; they are almost impossible to remove. Exposure of a tattoo and use of body jewelry is your personal business and should not be done on company time.

Body piercing: No studs, eye or nose rings or multiple ear piercings. This fad is on the wane. There is no place for it for interviewing or professional jobs where there are important client dealings, business meetings and contact with the public. It is not something you want to detract from your ability to perform and be taken seriously. You don't find CEOs walking around with a stud in the tongue or an eye ring. Neither should you.

Accessories for women

Jewelry: Limit how many pieces you wear at a given time. You don't want your jewelry to detract from your professional image. Here's a good rule: No more than five or six items at a time, so start counting with a pair of glasses, earrings, necklace, watch, ring (one per hand) and bracelet. Any more and it becomes overbearing and distracting.

- ☐ Keep the colors similar, gold, silver or a combination of both, in classic styles. Jewelry and accessories are to help finish off your outfit, not become the focal point of it.

- ☐ Keep your watch case thin, white or gold face, with or without a sweep hand. You can have a bracelet wristband but keep it light so it doesn't make noise. Do you know that a metal bracelet can fray the edge of your jacket, blouse or knit sleeves and cuffs? It is best to pick a leather watchband.

- ☐ If you wear a wedding ring, it is a dominant piece on its own and the focal point of your jewelry. Wear only one ring per hand and keep the colors similar to your other jewelry.

- ☐ Wear tight loop earrings or studs, in a classic style, and in colors similar to the rest of your jewelry. Big hanging earrings are a distraction; wear them on your personal time.

- ☐ A bracelet should be lightweight, not make noise and be in a color similar to your other jewelry. If you decide to wear a bracelet, keep it similar in size to your watch. Both the watch and bracelet are optional.

- ☐ If you wear glasses, pick a frame that complements the shape of your face and hairstyle. The frame should have color, not be monochromatic, that leads right to your eyes. The lenses have to be clear so your eyes are seen, not hidden.

- ☐ If you choose to wear a blouse that needs cuff links, pick classic styles and similar colors that go well with your other jewelry. Cuff links are available with and without stones. If you decide to wear a pair, use this in your count so you do not have too many jewelry items on at a given time.

☐ If you decide to wear either a lapel pin or a broach, keep the size down so it doesn't cause a distraction. Choose colors similar to other jewelry you are wearing.

☐ Pick a chain or necklace, one or the other, not both at the same time. And if you choose a scarf, pick that instead of a chain or necklace. Anything more will be too much distraction around your face. Chain necklaces should be thin, not heavy, and understated. Should not make noise or draw attention. Pearls should be single-strand, simple and understated.

Umbrella: You have a choice of one that collapses or a long fixed style. Make sure the quality complements your outfit. A collapsible umbrella is good to have and keep in your briefcase if you get caught in an unexpected shower.

Briefcase/folio: Pick a classic style. You do not have to match colors to your belt or shoes. Either item is something you carry, not wear. Choose from leather, canvas or microfiber in tan, brown, black or burgundy. Make sure it is not too large or bulky.

Purse: Pick classic styles in Kip, aniline or calf-skin leathers and match to your shoes and belts. A purse is something you carry what is essential – it is something you wear. It is not a piece of luggage and should not be used for that purpose. A purse should be professional in appearance.

Hats: Should be classic and complement your coat, scarf and gloves. The color can be the same as your coat or a contrast. Black, charcoal, burgundy and navy are your core colors. Red, eggplant, ivory and dark taupe are other colors you can pick from. For professional and business casual, a fine wool brim hat would be a good choice.

If the weather is really cold and inclement, you can pick a knit hat that will keep you warm and look professional. Black, charcoal, ivory, navy, burgundy, taupe and eggplant are all good color choices.

Gloves: Pick gloves that look professional and protect your hands. You can choose unlined glove styles that include the following choices of leather: matisse, glove, calf, deerskin, aniline or lambskin. If you choose lined leather gloves, your choice of linings include those made out of shearling, cashmere, rabbit fur or Thinsulate. Black is the predominant color choice. Other colors include gray, taupe, ivory, tan and brown. Select the color that is going to go with most of your coats.

Scarves: Choose long narrow styles that cover your neck, keep you warm and look professional. You can pick solid or pattern scarves. If you pick a pattern, keep it muted and in colors that complement your coat, hat and gloves. Merino and lamb's wool are warm and durable. If either of these wools gets wet, it won't mat down like cashmere or camel hair will.

If you choose cashmere or camel hair, wear only when it is cold and dry outside; otherwise, if they get wet, the fabrics can get ruined. The following solid colors are excellent choices: black, burgundy, navy, charcoal, gray, oatmeal, ivory, taupe and tan. When picking a scarf, choose a color or colors that will go with most of your outerwear.

16

All Dressed Up: Formal Apparel for Men and Women

*O*ur daughter is getting married to my largest client's son. I want her wedding to be perfect, but I also want to impress my client – thank you so much for adding this chapter about how to dress professionally for formal occasions! Priceless advice.

– Bill and Kathleen K., retired accountants

When the event calls for Black Tie, there is no substitute for a tuxedo. If you have to rent and wear a tuxedo more than twice a year, it will pay you to invest in one. Owning a tux will pay for itself in a short period of time.

Tuxedos are available right off the rack or made-to-measure. They are manufactured by the formalwear or men's clothing industry. Don't buy a tuxedo because of a name brand or designer label. Buy a tux for the quality of the fabric and the fit to your frame.

Prices vary from cheap to very expensive. Fabrics used can be polyester, wool, mohair or silk, and the quality can run from very cheap to outstanding.

The majority of tuxedo coat styles are a regular suit jacket coat length, single or double-breasted. Lapel styles can be a shawl, notch or peak lapel. The jackets are made with one, two, three or four button styles. Most are made in black, sometimes in a pattern or in white.

There are other fancy weaves and variations, but for the purpose of this book, we will concentrate on what works the majority of the time.

There are very good tuxedos made in opening to mid-level price ranges for men.

☐ Black superfine wool one-button single-breasted, notch, peak or shawl satin or grosgrain lapel, non-vent, besom pockets (no pocket flaps).

☐ Black superfine wool two- or three-button single-breasted, notch satin or grosgrain lapel, non-vent, besom pockets (no pocket flaps)

☐ Black superfine wool flat or pleated front slack, with satin or grosgrain waist (no belt loops) and on the outside leg seam. If you cannot keep your pants up, use button in black formal braces made of leather, rayon or silk.

☐ White superfine cotton, plain or pleated front shirt and a wing or lay collar. There are cuff options, but it is best to opt for French cuffs.

☐ Black bow tie and cummerbund set for a good basic color. Silver or red are other solid color options. You can also pick other solid color sets or pattern sets are an option. A lay down or wing collar works well with a bow tie and cummerbund set.

☐ Windsor tie and vest set is another alternative to a bow tie and cummerbund. The Windsor tie and vest looks best when worn with a lay down collar style shirt. Black, silver, red solid sets are all good choices. Pattern sets are available in a wide variety of colors as alternative choices.

☐ Formal cuff link set with studs. The studs are used instead of buttons to close the front of your shirt. Whatever you pick, keep the color the same as the rest of your jewelry. Cuff link sets are available in gold, silver or gold and silver combinations, with or without diamonds or other stones. There are all kinds of sets available from classic to flamboyant. Classic simple styles always look good and last and don't get dated.

☐ Black formal braces, in rayon, silk or leather. Leather will last for a long time. Braces are optional, but if you cannot keep your slacks from falling down, it is best if you wear braces; choose braces that button in, not clip on, the waist band.

☐ Black formal socks made of a fine-gauge wool or cotton. Silk is another option. Make sure the sock length comes up to your knee.

☐ Black patent leather shoe in either a plain toe slip-on or tie shoe

There are many options, but these timeless classics can be worn over and over again.

For a Black Tie event, women have a number of options such as a white or black sequined gown, white jacket over black evening pants or a black matte long sleeve jewel neck top and pant or a skirt.

Formal wear jackets include sequined, sweater, velvet, multi-colored woven raised textured weaves in nondescript, or paisley weaves. There are black tuxedos for women made from polyester or microfiber, velvet, superfine wools and silk.

Whatever you pick, make sure it is classic styling, understated and appropriate for your formal event. You will want to look your best.

☐ Black matte (microfiber or polyester) solid long-sleeve jewel neck top and a pull-on flat front black matte slack or long no waist skirt. The fabric flows and drapes to the body and has an elegant classic look.

☐ Black and white fancy, solid black or white woven, sequined or superfine wool or silk jacket in a jewel neck cardigan jacket worn over a black evening slack made of silk, silk and wool, velvet or matte.

☐   Sequined multi-color sweater jacket worn over a long black skirt or evening slack

☐   Black or white sequined gown made with an optional jacket

☐   Solid white or black spaghetti strap camisole made of silk charmeuse or microfiber

☐   Solid ivory, white or black silk charmeuse, silk or microfiber point collar French cuff blouse

☐   Strand of pearls, gold or silver pendant necklace, matching earrings (similar to the strand of pearls or necklace), watch, ring and bracelet. Keep the colors and size similar to each other. These items complete your outfit and create a very elegant look for you.

☐   Small black, white or gold purse. Keep the size just big enough to carry what you need to have for the evening, and keep the color similar to what you are wearing.

☐   Pair of white or black hosiery in solid or fancy weaves. There are metallic or speckled versions available.

☐   Pair of black matte (microfiber) or patent leather, plain toe, black bow or gold buckle pumps. Formal slip-on shoes are available in plain, cap toe, black ribbon or gold buckle in patent leather, matte or micro-suede styles.

Here are a couple of tuxedo tips for the fathers of the bride and groom. Nothing is more important than your child's wedding day! It is important to look your best. If the bridal party is wearing a tux, it is important for you to wear one as well. It is not only important for the ceremony but for the wedding pictures that will display cherished memories for years to come.

When everyone is not dressed consistently, appearance sticks out like a sore thumb. Dads normally dress in the same tux, shirt and shoes as the best man, groomsmen and ushers. The vest and tie can be different to distinguish you as Dad. Remember this is your day too, a proud moment you waited for. Look your best to share your joy.

If you have your own tux, make sure it fits well and goes reasonably well with the bridal party tuxedos. If you don't own one, rent one. Make sure you are fit correctly in a rental so you achieve a comfortable appearance for the wedding.

17

Away From the Office:
Conventions/Company
Meetings/Resort Wear

Whether I'm working at a convention or
trade show or I'm attending one at a resort
– it's tough to dress right. The information about
how to look great and be comfortable is going to
make a difference in how I am perceived. I should
know; I spend 30 weeks a year offsite at business
functions.

– Ray E.

In any setting away from the workplace, when you are representing
your company in front of vendors or especially clients, your dress
needs to be appropriate, adaptive and consistent. You may need
to wear everything from suits to shorts. So you need to make sure
whatever you wear, you make a smooth transition that enhances your
dress and image.

Never let your guard down. In any of these situations, you need to
know the business and social protocol in advance of your attendance.

It is sad to say, this is where people let themselves literally fall off a cliff. This is not time to dress sloppily where anything goes – even in Vegas.

For formal business meetings away from the office, the expectation is usually a suit. When you are attending an event, it is safest to ask the event coordinator what is proper dress. For most away conventions, business meetings and island resorts, dress is business casual, casual or resort wear.

Business casual and casual have already been defined, but what is resort wear? Similar to casual wear, resort wear will be a combination of the following:

An optional relaxed sport coat in a textured weave or in a solid or nondescript weave in a medium to a light or bright shade. The fabric can be silk, bamboo or a combination of silk and bamboo, cool wool (lightweight superfine wool and hard finish weave, this helps so the jacket will not wrinkle), microfiber, tencel or a combination of tencel/cotton/wool.

Linen is another option, but it wrinkles, does not hold its shape, will shrink and does not hold color well. Linen jackets are often found in semi or unconstructed models.

Shirts and blouses can be a tone-on-tone solid, made of silk, microfiber or some combination of cotton/silk, linen/cotton, tencel/cotton. The style of shirt is one that can be tucked in or worn out over a relaxed slack, skirt or short.

Soft tops in a crew or polo style, short-sleeve made of silk, micro-fiber, Pima cotton, tencel or a combination of silk and cotton, tencel and cotton or tencel and microfiber. Non-iron cotton pique polos, poplin, or twill short sleeve shirts are also available.

Soft tops are available in solid or fancy weaves. Silk shirts are available in solid tone-on-tone, floral and geometric weaves. Colors can be dark to light in vivid colors and shades.

Silk short-sleeve button front shirts (camp style) or blouses are excellent choices in solids or patterns. They stand on their own or work well underneath a jacket. The fabric drapes and doesn't cling and works well over a slack, skirt or short.

Slacks, skirts and shorts should be made of fabrics that hold their shape, drape and fit well and don't cling. Superfine worsted wool with stretch, microfiber, tencel and microfiber, silk, silk and cotton and tencel and microfiber are excellent fabrics.

MEN

Jacket

- ☐ Solid navy, black, natural, medium French blue blazer, cool wool or silk, raised textured or mini bone weave, two or three-button model, made in a center, side or no vent, pipe and flap or besom pockets. Select a single-breasted model.

- ☐ Fancy or nondescript silk or silk and wool sport coat. Color examples: black and white or ivory mix, black and white or ivory and blue or black and olive are good combinations for mix-and-match, two or three-button, single-breasted, in a center, side or no vent model.

Slacks

- ☐ Slacks in bone, natural, black, tan, navy or French blue, pleated or flat front model, in any of the following fabrics, superfine worsted stretch wool, microfiber, silk, tencel, blends of silk and wool, tencel and wool or tencel and microfiber weave. The slacks can be solid or a fancy pattern.

Shorts

- ☐ Solid shorts, pleated or flat front, knee length, solid or fancy weave, made of silk, wool, tencel, blends of silk and wool, tencel and cotton, tencel and microfiber, microfiber and wrinkle free or non-iron cotton.

Shirts

- ☐ Solid, tone-on-tone or print, short-sleeve camp style shirt made of silk or microfiber. Any fabric you select, make sure the material has good weight, drapes and does not cling. Make sure when you put it on the shirt complements the rest of your outfit. Pick medium or dark jewel tones and basic colors. Ivory, black, navy, melon, berry, tan, khaki, taupe and olive are good colors because they stand on their own or work well for mix-and-match.

- ☐ Solid or nondescript pattern polo made of silk, microfiber, mercerized and non-iron cotton, flat or pique weave, short sleeve with an open bottom and sleeve hem. The following colors work well for mix-and-match: white, black, French blue, olive, ivory, melon, apple green, soft yellow, denim blue, berry, taupe or tan.

Belt

Match your belt to your shoes, do not mix colors. If your shoes have a combination of colors, get a shade that matches best to the dominant color. There are belts made in raised weaves with one or more colors.

- ☐ Black and tan or brown, or tan and brown combination, solid or embossed weave, 1 to 1 ⅛ inches wide, gold or a silver buckle

Socks

- ☐ Solid or pattern sock, over-the-calf or slack length, made of fine-gauge Merino or mercerized cotton. If you are wearing darker colored slacks or shorts, pick darker color socks. If you are wearing lighter color slacks or shorts, pick lighter colors like tan, taupe or ivory.

Shoes

☐ Black, tan or black and tan color combination, plain or kiltie tassel slip-on, calf-skin, aniline or waxhide leather. The soles of your shoes can be vibram or a leather and vibram combination.

☐ Deck or boat shoe, waxhide leather, rubber sole, slip-on or lace-up style. Colors can be black, ivory or tan. Other color choices include blue, green, silver, rose, yellow or melon.

Outerwear

When attending business meetings and conventions and the dress is professional and the weather is cold and wet, use your microfiber or cotton all-weather coat. For business casual, use either your all-weather coat or a microfiber fingertip length (just above the thigh) jacket.

If you are in a warm weather climate for a meeting or convention, take a lightweight poplin cotton or microfiber solid colored chino, tan, stone or black jacket. In case of frequent tropical showers, you will protect your outfit. If you are going to wear a sport jacket, make sure the outerwear you pick will be long enough to cover the jacket.

WOMEN

Jacket

☐ Solid blazer or nondescript sport jacket made of a superfine worsted wool, microfiber or silk, in a two or three-button single-breasted model, with a non-vent, and pipe and flap or besom pocket. Navy, black, ivory, taupe, French blue, melon and grass green are all good options for different colored blazers.

☐ Pattern jackets made in silk or silk and wool can include the following color combinations: black and ivory, black and ivory and blue and black and taupe and olive in a "salt and pepper" or micro-screen weave.

Slack/skirt

☐ Solid slack in a stretch wool, microfiber, silk, silk and wool or triple stretch (nylon, polyester and spandex), in a flat front or pleated model. The fabric can be a flat or textured weave. Basic colors include black, navy, ivory, tan, taupe and olive. Your other color choices include French blue, soft yellow, sage, wheat, melon and berry. Any of these slack or skirt colors work well for mix-and-match and can be worn with or without a sport jacket.

☐ Fancy weave or nondescript silk or silk and wool slack in a flat front or pleated model. Colors can be black and tan, taupe, black and blue, black and sage or blue, sage and tan. The pattern can be a "salt and pepper" or a micro-screen weave.

☐ A skirt is optional. If you choose to wear one, the colors can be the same as the slacks, solid or pattern, mid- or calf-length, darted or with soft tucks and a back kick pleat. Choice of fabric can be a superfine stretch wool, microfiber, silk or silk and wool.

Shorts

☐ Solid or fancy solid (herringbone or tone-on-tone weave), flat front or pleated, in a cotton, cotton/tencel, cotton/microfiber, silk, microfiber or tencel knee length. Basic colors include black, navy, stone, chino, tan, khaki and ivory. Bright colors include grass green, melon, berry, yellow and cobalt blue.

Shirt/shell/polo

- ☐ Solid fancy silk or microfiber, short sleeve camp style shirt. Black, navy, taupe, ivory, yellow, sage, French blue, melon and berry are good color choices.

- ☐ Short sleeve shell, silk or microfiber, jewel or crew-neck, solid or fancy. Navy, black, ivory, taupe, sage, berry, cobalt, melon, yellow and tan are excellent color choices.

- ☐ Polo in a solid or fancy, short sleeve, silk or cotton. Your color choices include navy, black, white, ivory and yellow. Other choices include sage, melon, berry, tan and taupe.

Belt

If you choose to wear a belt (it is optional), match the color to your shoes and purse. If your shoes have more than one color, match to the dominant color. Belts are available in combinations of one or more colors in a raised textured weave, black or tan or black and tan combination, solid or embossed, ¾ to 1 inch width, gold or silver buckle.

Purse

If you carry a purse, make it leather, keep it small, just big enough to carry what you need and match it to your shoes and belt.

Hosiery

If you choose to wear a skirt and you are attending business meetings, do not go bare legged. If open-toed sandals are permitted, this may be an exception, so make sure you know well in advance. Otherwise wear neutral hose and closed-toe shoes with your skirt.

For slacks, select socks that are solid or have a small pattern that are slack length. Keep the colors similar to your slacks. Choose lightweight superfine cotton for your resort wear socks in black, navy, tan, taupe, ivory, sage, melon, berry, solid or pattern.

Shoes

For professional appearance, choose closed-toe shoes. The exception would be if open-toed sandals or shoes were permitted. Find out in advance of your attendance so you know how to plan.

Match your shoes to your belt, if you wear one, and your purse. Slip-ons and deck shoes are good choices for your resort wear outfits. Shoes can come in one or more colors; select colors that go with a majority of your outfits. The best choices are black, tan, black and tan combination, ivory, navy and taupe slip-on loafer, plain or tassel, leather, vibram or leather and vibram sole

Outerwear

If you are attending a convention or business meeting in a cold, wet climate, wear your microfiber or cotton all-weather coat. If the climate is warm, then select a lightweight jacket to protect you from any rain. Make sure the length of your outerwear is long enough to cover the bottom of your sport jacket or the hem when wearing a skirt or dress. Choose one of the following colors: black, tan, taupe, chino, stone, cement, in a lightweight cotton or micro-fiber jacket.

18

Clothing Care: Dry Cleaning and Laundering

Excellent advice on how to care for my clothing investment! I'm just starting out in my career, so my clothes have to last a long time! Thank you.

– Corey K.

When you spend good money on a wardrobe, excessive dry cleaning will reduce the longevity of the garment by as much as six months to a year.

Do not over dry clean your clothing. Too much, and you will be replacing your wardrobe much more often. Never take a suit to the cleaners more than three or four times a year and always clean the top and bottom together. Clean separate blazers and sport coats no more than three to four times a year; Slacks and skirts that are separate and not part of a suit, clean from six to eight times a year.

Guidelines for Dry Cleaning

☐ If you don't clean your suits together, eventually the top and bottom will be different shades.

☐ When you pick up your dry cleaning at the cleaners, smell your items. If you smell nothing, it means everything is clean. If you smell dry cleaning residue, your clothes are not clean. Time to change cleaners.

Ask the following questions before you leave your clothes:

☐ Is the dry cleaning solvent used safe for the fabric, interfacing and lining?

☐ Is low temperature used?

☐ Is the dry cleaning fluid mixed with water?

☐ How many times a day is the dry cleaning fluid changed?

Good cleaners use low temperature, no water and change the dry cleaning fluid several times a day so clothing gets cleaned. That way your dry cleaning does not come back with everyone else's dirt. A good litmus test is to smell your cleaning when you pick it up; if you cannot smell anything, you have clean clothing.

TIP

If you perspire while wearing your suit jacket, you will need to let it air out. Turn the jacket completely inside out and hang it on a curved plastic or a wooden hanger. Hang it up out in the open in a dry room to let the lining dry. The next morning, turn the jacket back out, hang it up in your closet and let it rest for one or two days.

When you put your dry cleaning away, remove the plastic from any wool or luxury fiber item. Natural fiber has to breathe. If not allowed to breathe, it will dry out. If you are not going to wear an item for some time, make sure it goes in the closet dry cleaned, not dirty.

Moth holes can occur in wool, cashmere, camel hair, alpaca and other luxury natural fibers. Moths are attracted to dark, humid areas. They are drawn to garments that have been worn and are attracted to body perspiration and oil from the skin. This is most likely where damage will occur. To prevent this damage, make sure your garments are left open and free of plastic. Moths hate dry cleaned clothing.

Rule of thumb to follow: Dry-clean your garments when they lose their shape, have body odor, or are dirty or stained. Dry cleaning only when necessary will keep your wardrobe looking fresh without taking away from the longevity of your garments.

Make sure your clothing has a good press. Good pressing is the hallmark of a good dry cleaner.

Guidelines for Laundering

Good practices by the cleaners who launder your clothing will insure you get maximum wear out of your shirts and blouses.

Cotton shirts (professionally laundered)

Ask your laundry how many times a day the water is changed. You want your garments to get cleaned – not come back dirty. Ask if they use cold or hot water. Cold is better to insure there is no shrinkage. Launder a good quality cotton 80's two-ply pinpoint or cotton broadcloth shirt that needs to be ironed once a week and ask for little or no starch. By following this procedure, you extend the life of the fabric out to about 2½ to 3 years of wear. Calculate the TRUE COST of having a better quality garment longer against spending less and replacing the item more often.

If you request starch, it is best to use light only. Using medium to heavy or extra heavy will do the following: Over prolonged use will yellow the shirt. Starch will become embedded in the cotton and eventually make the cotton split. It will block the porous properties of the cotton; the fabric will not breathe.

Ask the laundry if they use a Hot Head form to press? The stand is perforated. It blows steam from the inside. Not only does it press the shirts, it gives a crisp professionally-pressed look when finished.

Ask your cleaners if they replace cracked or missing buttons when they see them. Buttons have come a long way. When buying your shirt, make sure it has a hard plastic button. Mother of Pearl buttons are nice, they don't last. After repeated laundering, when the hot head touches the button, it contracts on the button holes, which eventually breaks them. This is the reason why buttons crystallize when you go to button the shirt.

Ask your cleaner when they finish pressing shirts, if they hand press the shirt collar and the sleeve cuffs. If they do, you have a good dry cleaner and launderer that does quality work.

Non-iron cotton shirts

The best performing non-iron cotton shirts and blouses are 100 percent cotton in a pinpoint weave. Polyester and cotton blends will break down prematurely. Polyester is a synthetic and will shrink and ball up. It shrinks at a faster rate than cotton and can cause seams and edges to ripple.

The non-iron technology has come a long way since its introduction. The following is a good guide when washing these shirts at home:

Wash in cold water on the permanent cycle. Use mild laundry soap. If you wash with other shirts, wash only with shirts of the same color and maximum of two or three shirts at a time.

Immediately take the shirts out of the washer and put in the dryer and use a delicate permanent cycle for 15 to 20 minutes. Then take the shirts out and hang them up. These garments are ready to wear, with no ironing required.

Do not starch. It is not necessary. You can ruin the finish. The process is not to iron and it works.

You have a sizable investment in your wardrobe. You want to keep your clothes looking good and clean just enough to keep them that way.

Look inside your garments and see what the care instructions are for each of your garments. Understand what the symbols mean. At the end of this chapter, you'll find the international symbols for dry cleaning and laundering and what they mean. Communicate these instructions to the dry cleaner when you drop off your clothing.

Before you wash at home, understand the laundry directions for each of the garments you wash. Giving proper care both for your laundry and dry cleaning will not only keep your clothing looking good, they will last much longer.

Guide to Common Home Laundering and Drycleaning Symbols

The following pages are reprinted with permission from Textile Industry Affairs, www.textileaffairs.com. This site contains a vast amount of valuable information on the care of clothing and other textiles. To protect your investment in your clothes, review the information on this site and follow the guidelines.

GUIDE TO COMMON HOME LAUNDERING AND DRYCLEANING SYMBOLS

DOS/WIN Code Ref	Care Symbol	Written Care Instructions	What Care Symbol and Instructions Mean
Wash MW_Norm		Machine Wash, Normal	Garment may be laundered through the use of hottest available water, detergent or soap, agitation, and a machine designed for this purpose.
MW30C	30C	Machine Wash, Cold	Initial water temperature should not exceed 30C or 65 to 85F.
MW40C	40C	Machine Wash, Warm	Initial water temperature should not exceed 40C or 105F.
MW50C	50C	Machine Wash, Hot	Initial water temperature should not exceed 50C or 120F.
MW60C	60C	Machine Wash, Hot	Initial water temperature should not exceed 60C or 140F.
MW70C	70C	Machine Wash, Hot	Initial water temperature should not exceed 70C or 160F.
MW95C	95C	Machine Wash, Hot	Initial water temperature should not exceed 95C or 200F.
MW_Pres		Machine Wash, Permanent Press	Garment may be machine laundered only on the setting designed to preserve Permanent Press with cool down or cold rinse prior to reduced spin.
MW Gentl		Machine Wash, Gentle or Delicate	Garment may be machine laundered only on the setting designed for gentle agitation and/or reduced time for delicate items.
Hndw		Hand Wash	Garment may be laundered through the use of water, detergent or soap and gentle hand manipulation.
W_DoNot		Do Not Wash	Garment may not be safely laundered by any process. Normally accompanied by Dry Clean instructions.
Bleach B_Any		Bleach When Needed	Any commercially available bleach product may be used in the laundering process.
B_NonChl		Non-Chlorine Bleach When Needed	Only a non-chlorine, color-safe bleach may be used in the laundering process. Chlorine bleach may not be used.
B_DoNt_S		Do Not Bleach	No bleach product may be used. The garment is not colorfast or structurally able to withstand any bleach.

NOTE: SYSTEM OF DOTS INDICATING TEMPERATURE RANGE IS THE SAME FOR ALL WASH PROCEDURES.

NOTE: All (98+%) washable textiles are safe in some type of bleach. IF BLEACH IS NOT MENTIONED OR REPRESENTED BY A SYMBOL ANY BLEACH MAY BE USED.

Distributed by: TEXTILE INDUSTRY AFFAIRS / 800-424-5514 Fax: 843-449-9845 Email: Info@TextileAffairs.com

Page 1

GUIDE TO COMMON HOME LAUNDERING AND DRYCLEANING SYMBOLS

DOS/WIN Code Ref#	Care Symbol	Written Care Instructions	What Care Symbol and Instructions Mean
Dry TD_Nor	⊙	**Tumble Dry, Normal**	A machine dryer may be regularly used at the hottest available temperature setting.
TD_Nor_L	⊙	**Tumble Dry, Normal, Low Heat**	A machine dryer may be regularly used at a maximum of Low Heat setting.
TD_Nor_M	⊙	**Tumble Dry, Normal, Medium Heat**	A machine dryer may be regularly used at a maximum of Medium Heat setting.
TD_Nor_H	⊙	**Tumble Dry, Normal, High Heat**	A machine dryer may be regularly used at a High Heat setting.
TD_NoHel	●	**Tumble Dry, Normal, No Heat**	A machine dryer may be regularly used only at No Heat or Air Only setting.
TD_PP	⊙	**Tumble Dry, Permanent Press**	A machine dryer may be regularly used only at the Permanent Press setting.
TD_Gen_L	⊙	**Tumble Dry, Gentle**	A machine dryer may be regularly used only at the Gentle setting.
TD_DoNot	⊠	**Do Not Tumble Dry**	A machine dryer may not be used. Usually accompanied by an alternate drying method symbol.
Dr_DoNot	⊠	**Do Not Dry**	A machine dryer may not be used. Usually accompanied by an alternate drying method symbol.
Dry_Line	⬜	**Line Dry**	Hang damp garment from line or bar, in or out doors.
Dr_Drip	⫴	**Drip Dry**	Hang dripping wet garment from line or bar, in or out doors, without hand shaping or smoothing
Dr_Flat	⊟	**Dry Flat**	Lay out horizontally for drying.
Dr_Shade	◩	**Dry In Shade**	Usually added to Line or Drip Dry. Dry away from direct sunlight.
Wring Wr_DoNot	⋈	**Do Not Wring**	Do not wring.

NOTE
SYSTEM OF DOTS INDICATING TEMPERATURE RANGE IS THE SAME FOR ALL DRY PROCEDURES.

GUIDE TO COMMON HOME LAUNDERING AND DRYCLEANING SYMBOLS

DOS/WIN Code Ref#	Care Symbol	Written Care Instructions	What Care Symbol and Instructions Mean
Iron Ir_Tall		Iron, Any Temperature, Steam or Dry	Regular ironing may be needed and may be performed at any available temperature with or without steam is acceptable.
Ir_Tall_L		Iron, Low	Regular ironing, steam or dry, may be performed at Low setting (110C, 230F) only.
Ir_Tall_M		Iron, Medium	Regular ironing, steam or dry, may be performed at Medium setting (150C, 300F).
Ir_Tall_H		Iron, High	Regular ironing, steam or dry, may be performed at High setting (200C, 290F).
Ir_NoStm		Do Not Steam	Steam ironing will harm garment, but regular dry ironing at indicated temperature setting is acceptable.
Ir_DoNt		Do Not Iron	Item may not be smooted or finished with an iron.

NOTE SYSTEM OF DOTS INDICATING TEMPERATURE RANGE IS THE SAME FOR ALL IRONING PROCEDURES.

NOTE: IF IRONING IS NOT A NECESSARY, REGULAR CARE PROCEDURE IT NEED NOT BE MENTIONED.

DOS/WIN Code Ref#	Care Symbol	Written Care Instructions	What Care Symbol and Instructions Mean
Dryclean DC_Circle		Dryclean	Dry Clean, any solvent, any cycle any moisture, any heat.
DC_A		Dryclean, Any Solvent	Dry Clean, any solvent. Usually used with other restrictions on proper dry cleaning procedure.
DC_F		Dryclean, Petroleum Solvent Only	Dry Clean using only petroleum solvent. Usually used with other restrictions.
DC_P		Dryclean, Any Solvent Except Trichloroethylene	Any dry cleaning solvent other than trichloroethylene may be safely used.
DC_S_Cyc		Dryclean, Short Cycle	May be used with A, P, or F solvent restriction.
DC_RMois		Dryclean, Reduced Moisture	May be used with A, P, or F solvent restriction.
DC_LHet		Dryclean, Low heat	May be used with A, P, or F solvent restriction.
DC_NSt		Dryclean, No Steam	May be used with A, P, or F solvent restriction.
DC_DoNot		Do Not Dryclean	Garment may not be commercially drycleaned.

19

A Wardrobe for Life:
What to Buy Now and
What to Buy Next

Your breakdown of What to Buy Now, What to
Buy Next and Other Options literally lifted the
spirits of the career center. We had a class about
professional dress versus business casual planned,
and one of my students brought this book. I would
like to add it to my classroom as required reading.
Nice presentation and very easy to read and
understand. I appreciate your work very much!
                        – Sherry H., Ph.D., Long Island

Acquire a never-forgotten image!

A Wardrobe for Life is what you wear daily, it defines your daily
image and appearance, from the interview to a resort meeting. This
chapter offers examples of what to buy now and a suggested order
for other items to help you get the most from your wardrobe as you
build it. Following these suggestions will help you mix-and-match
outfits through the workweek as you add pieces.

You don't want to appear to be wearing the same clothing every day; the following examples will show how to make the most of what you have. This is how you make your wardrobe work for you and realize the "dividends" of a well-thought-out wardrobe.

You cannot buy everything at once nor should you; wardrobe building doesn't happen overnight – it takes time!

Eventually, your clothing starts to get old or wear out and is replaced by new items, enabling two things to happen – #1 you don't have the major expense of replacing an entire wardrobe all at once – because you have been adding as needed through the year – #2 everything doesn't wear out at once.

Buy the best quality you can afford, your wardrobe will last longer and you'll spend less in the long run. You will have clothing you can dress up or down and be worn year round. This is the true return-on-investment your wardrobe will afford you.

Remember there is no free lunch; you have to match quality with value. If something is cheaply made, you will be replacing that item rather than adding to your wardrobe – this is what makes buying clothing very expensive.

When you are just starting out, you have everything coming at you. Allow plenty of time to search for your wardrobe. Plan enough time before you need to actually wear your new garment to enable you to shop in all kinds of stores for a variety of quality items. Besides large stores and chains, there are many fine specialty stores that are no more expensive.

You may find the individual attention you want and get to work with people who take your interest to heart and will work with you to achieve the results you seek. There are many options – stores specializing in wardrobe building exist and are staffed with experts, not just clerks.

A store can be only as good as its people. There are many fine dedicated people who are professionals at what they do – these are the people who can help you. Finding a professional who knows fabrics, fit and how to mix-and-match a smart wardrobe is key.

Never judge a book by its cover and the same goes for stores. Discover new stores, open their door or make a phone call. Putting your wardrobe together is serious (and expensive) business.

One store cannot stock everything. What you need may not be stocked or currently available. Depending on the time of year it may be out of stock, the change of seasons, or any number of other reasons. Special orders may be an option. Not only do you need the time to find the stores and the items you need, but you need to allow enough time for alterations. In the end a well-planned wardrobe shows.

Below are core recommendations to begin your wardrobe. Nothing is set in stone. Any purchase you make should be based on your needs. The following are examples you can use as a guide to planning your wardrobe.

The suggested items are targeted to build your wardrobe fairly quickly, mix-and-match and make your wardrobe function – to get more outfits out of what you have and do it without wasting money.

PROFESSIONAL WARDROBE FOR MEN

Professional Dress (Interview): Suit colors of business navy, black and gray as your primary colors and very important for the interview. Have enough clothing to get you through the Interview process – these will be the same garments you will transition to your new career.

If the job you seek requires a suit for daily wear or three or four times a week, you'll want to have these items in your wardrobe:

Buy now:

- ☐ 1 black solid wool 2 or 3 button single-breasted, flat front or pleated model suit
- ☐ 2 white point collar or hidden button down cotton – iron or non-iron shirts
- ☐ 2 to 3 solid or pattern ties.
- ☐ 1 black leather belt or a pair of braces

- ☐ 1 black tie plain, cap or panel toe style shoe with a leather or combination sole
- ☐ 1 black solid or pattern, Merino wool or cotton lisle over-the-calf pair of socks

Buy next:

- ☐ 1 navy solid wool 2 or 3 button single-breasted, flat front or pleated model suit
- ☐ 1 medium or deep blue solid, point or hidden button down collar, iron or non-iron cotton long sleeve shirt
- ☐ 1 or 2 more solid or pattern ties in other colors
- ☐ 1 additional black belt or braces
- ☐ 1 additional black tie plain, cap or panel toe style shoe with a leather or combination sole
- ☐ 1 pair of solid or pattern black, Merino or cotton lisle, over-the-calf socks

Options for Professional Dress as You Add Pieces

- ☐ 1 navy pinstripe superfine wool suit, tic weave or a birdseye weave, 2 or 3-button single-breasted, none, side or center vent and flat front or pleated slack
- ☐ 1 charcoal gray solid, micro-screen, mini herringbone, sharkskin or stripe superfine wool suit, 2 or 3 button single-breasted suit, none, side or center vent, plain or pleated slack
- ☐ 1 white and blue or burgundy pinstripe or graph check cotton, point or hidden button down collar, iron or non-iron shirt
- ☐ 1 burgundy belt or pair of braces
- ☐ 1 burgundy tie plain, cap or panel toe style shoe with a leather or combination sole
- ☐ 1 pair charcoal gray solid or pattern, over-the-calf, Merino or cotton lisle socks

BUSINESS CASUAL WARDROBE
FOR MEN (Interview)

Buy now:

- ☐ 1 navy solid superfine wool 2 or 3 button single-breasted blazer
- ☐ 1 charcoal solid superfine slack, flat front or pleated
- ☐ 1 taupe solid superfine slack, flat front or pleated
- ☐ 1 blue or ink blue cotton solid or fancy long-sleeve shirt, iron, non-iron or wrinkle free, point, hidden or button-down collar
- ☐ 1 white and navy stripe or graph check cotton, iron, non-iron or wrinkle free, point, hidden button down or button down collar shirt
- ☐ 1 black tie shoe, leather or combination sole, solid, cap or panel toe style
- ☐ 1 black solid or embossed leather belt
- ☐ 1 black solid or pattern over-the-calf pair of socks, cotton lisle or Merino wool blend
- ☐ 1 taupe solid or pattern over-the-calf pair of socks, cotton lisle or Merino wool blend

Buy next:

- ☐ 1 black solid superfine wool 2 or 3 button single-breasted blazer
- ☐ 1 khaki (tan) or mid gray superfine wool solid slack, flat or pleated model
- ☐ 1 ivory (off white) or ecru (egg shell color) solid or fancy long-sleeve cotton shirt, iron, non-iron or wrinkle free, point, hidden button down or button down
- ☐ 1 white and burgundy stripe or graph check long sleeve cotton, iron, non-iron or wrinkle free, point, hidden button or button down shirt

- ☐ 1 mid-tan tie shoe, leather or combination sole, plain, cap or panel toe style
- ☐ 1 mid-tan solid or embossed leather belt
- ☐ 1 khaki (tan) or mid gray solid or pattern over-the-calf sock, cotton lisle or Merino wool blend

Options:

- ☐ 1 multi-tic or micro-screen pattern, wool or silk and wool blend, 2 or 3 button single-breasted sport coat
- ☐ 1 white, melon, rose or ecru multi colored window pane, graph check or stripe cotton, iron, non-iron or wrinkle free, point, hidden button down or button down long sleeve shirt
- ☐ 1 olive solid superfine wool flat front or pleated slack
- ☐ 1 black solid superfine wool flat front or pleated slack to go with a fancy or pattern sport coat

CASUAL WARDROBE FOR MEN (Interview)

Buy now:

- ☐ 1 blue or ink blue, solid or pattern, long-sleeve, iron, non-iron or wrinkle free cotton, point, hidden button down or button down collar shirt
- ☐ 1 white solid or pattern, long-sleeve, iron, non-iron or wrinkle free cotton, point, hidden button down or button down collar shirt
- ☐ 1 khaki or mid-tan slack, cotton twill, pleated or flat front, wrinkle free or non-iron cotton
- ☐ 1 black slack, cotton twill, pleated or flat front, wrinkle free.
- ☐ 1 black belt, solid or embossed

- ☐ 1 black tie shoe, plain, cap or panel toe style, combination sole
- ☐ 1 khaki or mid-tan pair of socks, slack length (longer than anklet length), cotton lisle or Merino wool, solid or pattern
- ☐ 1 black pair of socks, slack length, cotton lisle or Merino wool, solid or pattern

Note: Short-sleeve shirts and polos are optional, but long sleeve shirts have a professional appearance. Before showing up to an interview, inquire about wearing a short sleeve shirt or polo.

If short sleeve shirts are permitted (normally between Memorial to Labor Day) use the same solid and pattern colors, collar styles and iron, non-iron or wrinkle free fabrics for short sleeve shirts.

Buy next:

- ☐ 1 ivory, ecru or tan polo, short-sleeve, solid, iron or non-iron cotton pique weave
- ☐ 1 melon or rose polo, short-sleeve, solid, iron or non-iron cotton pique weave
- ☐ 1 ivory or ecru multi-patterned (colors that go with several slacks) shirt, iron, non-iron or wrinkle free, point, hidden button down or button down
- ☐ 1 melon or light green solid or multi-patterned, iron, non-iron or wrinkle free cotton shirt, point, hidden button or button down collar
- ☐ 1 olive cotton twill (non-iron or wrinkle free), superfine wool or microfiber solid slack, flat front or pleated
- ☐ 1 taupe microfiber or superfine wool solid slack, flat front or pleated
- ☐ 1 mid tan slip on shoes, combination sole, plain, panel, tassel or kiltie style. The other option is a tie shoe in a plain, cap or panel style

Optional:

- ☐ 1 ecru or tan, solid or pattern, long-sleeve, iron, non-iron or wrinkle free cotton, point, hidden button down or button down collar shirt

- ☐ 1 melon solid or pattern, long-sleeve, iron, non-iron or wrinkle free cotton, point, hidden button down or button down collar shirt

- ☐ 1 white polo, short-sleeve, solid, iron or non-iron cotton pique weave

- ☐ 1 blue or cobalt blue polo, short-sleeve, solid, iron or non-iron cotton pique weave

- ☐ 1 pair of black slip-on shoes, combination sole, plain, panel, and tassel or kiltie style

- ☐ 1 black microfiber or superfine solid wool slack, flat front or pleated

- ☐ 1 taupe or khaki microfiber or superfine solid wool slack, flat front or pleated

- ☐ 1 chino or navy cotton twill, iron or non-iron, flat front or pleated slack

- ☐ 1 mid-gray, charcoal, navy or mid-brown microfiber or superfine wool, flat front or pleated slack

Note: If you are going to wear a short-sleeve shirt or polo for casual interviews, you will need to have enough shirts to rotate during the interview process.

PROFESSIONAL WARDROBE FOR WOMEN

Buy now:

- ☐ 1 black superfine wool or microfiber suit separates (that includes a jacket, skirt and flat front or pleated slack – to have for business casual), 1, 2 or 3 button single-breasted jacket and a mid-length skirt

- [ ] 2 white point collar long-sleeve, iron, non-iron or wrinkle free cotton blouses
- [ ] 1 small black clutch handbag
- [ ] 1 black classic closed toe plain or cap toe pump with a heel height of 1" to 1¼"
- [ ] 2 pair of quality neutral color panty hose

Buy next:

- [ ] 1 navy superfine wool or microfiber suit separates (that includes a jacket, skirt and flat front or pleated slack – to have for business casual), 1, 2 or 3 button single-breasted jacket and a mid-length skirt
- [ ] 1 white or ivory long sleeve crew-neck microfiber top
- [ ] 1 black solid or embossed leather belt
- [ ] 1 black plain or cap closed toe pump with a 1" to 1¼" heel height

Optional:

- [ ] 1 navy, black, or charcoal stripe superfine wool or microfiber suit with a 1, 2 or 3 button single-breasted jacket and a mid-length skirt
- [ ] 1 charcoal gray solid superfine wool or microfiber suit with a 1, 2 or 3 button single-breasted jacket and a mid-length skirt
- [ ] 1 taupe, eggplant or olive solid superfine wool or microfiber single-breasted skirt suit (when not interviewing)
- [ ] 1 blue, pink, or rose solid long sleeve point collar, iron, non-iron or wrinkle free cotton blouse
- [ ] 1 white and blue, red or burgundy stripe or graph check point collar cotton, iron, non-iron or wrinkle free blouse
- [ ] 1 burgundy closed toe pump, belt and handbag

BUSINESS CASUAL FOR WOMEN

Buy now:

- ☐ 1 black superfine wool or microfiber, 1, 2, or 3 button single-breasted blazer

- ☐ 1 taupe superfine wool or microfiber, flat front or pleated slack

- ☐ 1 white solid or tone-on-tone point collar, long sleeve, iron, non-iron or wrinkle cotton blouse

- ☐ 1 blue or ink blue solid or end-on-end point collar, long sleeve, iron, non-iron or wrinkle free cotton blouse

- ☐ 1 crew-neck or keyhole (one-button back closure) micro-fiber or silk, white, pink, rose, blue or melon shell

- ☐ 1 black solid or embossed leather belt

- ☐ 1 black closed toe plain or cap toe, 1" to 1 ¼" pumps

- ☐ 1 pair of taupe solid or pattern slack length Merino wool or cotton lisle socks

Optional:

- ☐ 1 multi-pattern tic or micro-screen wool or wool and silk, single-breasted, 1, 2, or 3 button sport jacket

- ☐ 1 multi colored salt and pepper or donegal weave silk or microfiber, single-breasted, 1, 2, or 3 button sport jacket

Buy next:

- ☐ 1 navy solid superfine wool or microfiber blazer, single-breasted, 1, 2, or 3 button blazer

- ☐ 1 white and blue, red or burgundy stripe or graph check, point collar long sleeve, iron, non-iron or wrinkle free cotton blouse

- ☐ 1 ivory, rose or ink blue multi colored pattern or stripe, point collar long sleeve, iron, non-iron or wrinkle free cotton blouse
- ☐ 1 charcoal gray superfine wool or microfiber, flat front or pleated slack
- ☐ 1 charcoal gray slack Merino wool or cotton lisle, solid or pattern socks (similar shade to slack)
- ☐ 1 black closed toe flat or loafer shoe

Optional:

- ☐ 1 khaki, olive or mustard solid or fancy weave superfine wool or microfiber, flat front or pleated slack
- ☐ 1 mid tan or burgundy solid or embossed leather belt
- ☐ 1 mid tan or burgundy closed toe loafer or pump with a 1" to 1 ¼" heel heigh

CASUAL WOMEN (Interview)

Buy now:

- ☐ 1 white solid or pattern long sleeve point collar, iron, non-iron or wrinkle free cotton blouse
- ☐ 1 blue or ink blue solid or end-on-end pattern long sleeve point collar, iron, non-iron or wrinkle free cotton blouse
- ☐ 1 ecru, blue, melon or rose solid or pattern long sleeve point collar, iron, non-iron or wrinkle free blouse
- ☐ 1 black stretch flat front or pleated superfine wool or microfiber slack
- ☐ 1 taupe stretch flat front or pleated superfine wool or microfiber slack
- ☐ 1 black solid or embossed leather belt

☐   1 black tie or loafer style shoe

☐   1 black cotton lisle solid or pattern slack length socks

☐   1 taupe cotton lisle solid or pattern slack length socks

Optional:

☐   1 black cotton wrinkle-resistant flat front or pleated slack

☐   1 tan cotton wrinkle-resistant flat front or pleated slack

Buy next:

☐   1 stone solid superfine wool or microfiber flat front or pleated slack

☐   1 olive solid superfine wool or microfiber flat front or pleated slack

☐   1 ivory, melon, tan or rose crew-neck or keyhole (one-button back closure) silk or microfiber top

☐   1 white or ivory multi-colored graph check point collar long sleeve, iron, non-iron or wrinkle free cotton blouse

☐   1 melon or olive multi-colored stripe or graph check point collar long sleeve, iron, non-iron or wrinkle free cotton blouse

☐   1 mid tan solid or embossed leather belt

☐   1 mid tan tie or loafer leather shoe

☐   1 stone cotton lisle solid or pattern slack length pair of socks

☐   1 olive cotton lisle solid or pattern slack length pair of socks

Optional:

☐   1 stone cotton wrinkle-resistant flat front or pleated slack

☐   1 olive cotton wrinkle-resistant flat front or pleated slack

- ☐ 1 wrinkle-resistant cotton pique or lisle solid short polo or iron, non-iron or wrinkle free cotton point collar solid or pattern short sleeve blouses (if permitted by your employer)
- ☐ 1 or 2 polos or short sleeve blouses to mix-and-match. White, melon, ivory, black, rose, pink, navy and cobalt blue are good colors to build with

BUSINESS EVENING FUNCTION FOR MEN

When the evening function does not require formal dress and is not necessarily business casual dress, what do you wear?

Buy now:

- ☐ 1 black single-breasted solid or tone-on-tone superfine wool, 2 or 3 button suit with a flat front or pleated slack
- ☐ 1 white solid or tone-on-tone, point or spread collar, button, convertible or french cuff shirt
- ☐ 1 black solid or pattern or black and white silk tie
- ☐ 1 black solid or embossed leather belt; solid or braid leather braces
- ☐ 1 black plain, cap or panel toe tie shoe
- ☐ 1 black solid or muted fancy pattern Merino, cotton lisle or silk over-the-calf socks

Option one:

- ☐ 1 solid black superfine wool, 2 or 3 button single-breasted blazer
- ☐ 1 charcoal gray solid superfine wool flat front or pleated slack

Option two:

- ☐ 1 black and white micro-screen superfine wool or silk, silk and wool donegal patter sport coat
- ☐ 1 black superfine wool flat front or pleated slack

BUSINESS EVENING FUNCTION FOR WOMEN

Buy now:

- ☐ 1 black dress made of microfiber, a matted polyester, a silk blend or a superfine wool that can be worn with a jacket, shawl or a wrap
- ☐ 1 black pump, 1" to 1 ½" heel height
- ☐ 1 neutral or black sheer panty hose

Optional:

- ☐ 1 or 2 black dresses made of microfiber, a matted polyester, silk blend or superfine wool that can be worn with a jacket, shawl or a wrap
- ☐ 1 black evening pant suit made of microfiber, a matted polyester, silk blend or superfine wool

BUSINESS MEETING/RESORT WEAR FOR MEN

Buy now:

- ☐ 1 semi-constructed relaxed sport coat in a solid black or nondescript fancy weave in a lightweight wool or silk and wool blend
- ☐ 2 or 3 button single-breasted model
- ☐ 1 black superfine wool, lightweight microfiber or a tencel blend flat front or pleated slack
- ☐ 1 ivory short sleeve solid or print silk camp style shirt

- ☐ 1 black embossed leather or linen belt
- ☐ 1 black loafer or deck shoe
- ☐ 1 black pair of pattern slack length cotton lisle socks

Optional:

- ☐ 1 solid ivory or French blue solid or fancy weave 2 or 3 button single-breasted sport coat
- ☐ 1 chino, stone or ivory solid superfine wool, lightweight microfiber or tencel blend flat front or pleated slack
- ☐ 1 short sleeve polo in a solid or fancy mercerized cotton in ivory, melon, rose, white, soft yellow or tan color
- ☐ 1 natural linen or tan color embossed belt
- ☐ 1 natural or tan loafer or deck shoe

Another option:

- ☐ If a sport coat isn't required and dress shorts are permitted: 1 black or natural solid or textured weave silk or microfiber flat front or pleated shorts.

BUSINESS MEETING/RESORT WEAR FOR WOMEN

Buy now:

- ☐ 1 relaxed black or ivory solid color blazer or nondescript fancy weave 2 or 3 button single-breasted model made of a superfine lightweight wool, silk, silk and wool or microfiber
- ☐ 1 solid color natural or black pleated or flat front slack made of a light superfine wool, microfiber, silk or tencel blend
- ☐ 1 black or ivory solid or fancy weave silk camp style blouse.
- ☐ 1 black or natural leather or linen belt

☐   1 black or natural loafer or deck shoe

☐   1 black or natural solid or pattern slack length cotton
     lisle pair of socks

Buy next:

☐   1 black and ivory silk and wool donegal or multi muted
     pattern 2 or 3 button single-breasted jacket

☐   1 French blue, melon or taupe solid blazer or textured weave
     2 or 3 button single-breasted sport coat

☐   1 chino or light tan superfine wool, lightweight microfiber,
     silk or tencel blend flat front or pleated slack

☐   1 lightweight short sleeve, solid or nondescript multi colored
     fancy weave mercerized polo

☐   1 mid tan solid or embossed leather or linen belt

☐   1 mid tan loafer or deck shoe

☐   1 chino or light tan slack length cotton lisle solid or fancy
     slack length pair of socks

Optional:

If a sport coat isn't required and dress shorts are permitted:

☐   1 black or natural lightweight microfiber, tencel blend or silk
     flat front or pleated knee length shorts

☐   As an alternative to slacks, a mid length black or natural
     colored skirt made of a lightweight superfine wool,
     lightweight microfiber or silk

"Know, first, who you are; and then adorn yourself accordingly."

— Epictetus

Men: Example of a Two-Week Rotation
For a Professional and Business Casual Wardrobe

WEEK ONE

Monday
Navy solid suit, white shirt, red pattern tie, black belt or braces, black solid socks and black tie shoes

Tuesday
Gray stripe suit, blue end-on-end shirt, burgundy pattern tie, burgundy belt or braces, gray pattern socks and burgundy shoes

Wednesday
Black solid suit, white and black stripe shirt, black pattern tie, black belt or braces, black solid socks and black shoes

Thursday
Navy stripe suit, solid blue shirt, blue pattern tie, black belt or braces, navy pattern socks and black shoes

Friday
Black suit jacket or separate blazer, charcoal gray slack, white and black graph check shirt, black pattern tie, black solid sock and black shoes

WEEK TWO

Monday
Gray solid suit, white and burgundy graph check shirt, burgundy solid tie, burgundy belt or braces, charcoal solid socks and burgundy shoes

Tuesday
Navy suit jacket or separate blazer, taupe slack, ecru solid shirt, navy and taupe multi-pattern tie, mid tan belt or braces, taupe pattern socks and mid tan shoes

Wednesday
Black stripe suit, white-on-white solid shirt, burgundy stripe tie, burgundy belt or braces, black pattern socks and burgundy tie shoes

Thursday
Olive tic weave suit, ecru solid shirt, olive solid socks, black belt or braces and black shoes

Friday
Black and taupe micro-screen sport coat, black slack, ivory fancy weave hidden button down shirt, black belt or braces, black pattern socks and black slip on shoes

For Saturday and Sunday, visit our Web site at www.DressLikeTheBigFish.com

Example of a
Men's Professional Wardrobe

- ☐ 1 - navy solid suit
- ☐ 1 - black solid suit
- ☐ 1 - charcoal gray stripe suit
- ☐ 1 - black stripe or pattern suit
- ☐ 1 - navy stripe or pattern suit
- ☐ 1 - charcoal solid suit
- ☐ 1 - black and white or black and tan micro-screen suit
- ☐ 3 - white solid shirts
- ☐ 1 - blue or ink blue solid shirt
- ☐ 1 - white and burgundy stripe shirt
- ☐ 1 - white and navy graph check shirt
- ☐ 1 - white and black stripe or graph check shirt
- ☐ 1 - burgundy solid or pattern tie
- ☐ 1 - eggplant pattern tie
- ☐ 1 - black pattern tie
- ☐ 1 - navy pattern tie
- ☐ 2 - pair of black tie shoes
- ☐ 2 - sets of cedar shoe trees
- ☐ 1 - leather belt or pair of braces
- ☐ 3 - pair of solid black or pattern socks
- ☐ 2 - pair of solid navy or pattern socks
- ☐ 2 - pair of solid charcoal gray or pattern socks

Example of a
Men's Business Casual Wardrobe

☐ 1 - navy solid blazer

☐ 1 - black solid blazer

☐ 1 - multi colored check, tic or micro-screen
pattern sport coat

☐ 1 - taupe solid slack

☐ 1 - black solid slack

☐ 1 - olive solid or fancy slack

☐ 1 - charcoal gray solid slack

☐ 1 - white solid or fancy long sleeve shirt

☐ 1 - blue solid or fancy long sleeve shirt

☐ 1 - tan solid or fancy long sleeve shirt

☐ 1 - rose solid or fancy long sleeve shirt

☐ 1 - mid-tan belt or braces

☐ 1 - black belt or braces

☐ 1 - mid-tan pair of shoes

☐ 2 - black pair of shoes

☐ 3 - pair of cedar shoe trees

☐ 2 - solid or pattern taupe socks

☐ 2 - solid or pattern charcoal socks

☐ 2 - solid or pattern black socks

Example of a
Men's Casual Wardrobe

☐ 2 - tan cotton, microfiber or wool solid slacks

☐ 1 - chino cotton or microfiber solid slacks

☐ 1 - gray microfiber or wool solid or fancy slack

☐ 1 - black cotton or microfiber solid slack

☐ 1 - black solid or fancy wool slack

☐ 1 - navy solid cotton or microfiber slack

☐ 1 - white multi colored check or stripe shirt

☐ 1 - ecru multi colored check or stripe shirt

☐ 1 - blue or ink blue solid or end-on-end shirt

☐ 1 - melon multi-colored shirt

☐ 1 - white solid or fancy shirt

☐ 3 - solid or fancy cotton white, ecru, blue or black polos

☐ 1 - melon or rose polo

☐ 1 - black belt

☐ 1 - mid tan belt

☐ 2 - pair of black shoes

☐ 1 - pair of mid tan shoes

☐ 3 - pair of cedar shoe trees

☐ 2 - black solid or fancy socks

☐ 2 - tan solid or fancy socks

☐ 2 - gray solid or fancy socks

*"Always be a first-rate version of yourself,
instead of a second-rate version of someone else."*
– Judy Garland

Women: Example of a Two-Week Rotation
For a Professional and Business Casual Wardrobe

WEEK ONE

Monday
Navy solid skirted suit, white blouse, necklace or strand of pearls, black belt (optional), neutral hose, black purse and black closed toe pump

Tuesday
Gray stripe or tic weave skirted suit, blue end-on-end blouse, necklace or strand or pearls, burgundy belt (optional), neutral hose, burgundy purse and burgundy closed toe pump

Wednesday
Black solid or pattern skirted suit, white and black stripe blouse, necklace or strand of pearls, black belt (optional), neutral hose, black purse and black closed toe pump

Thursday
Navy stripe skirted suit, solid blue blouse, necklace or strand of pearls, black belt (optional), neutral hose and black closed toe pump

Friday
Black suit jacket or separate solid blazer, gray solid or fancy weave slack, white and black graph check blouse, black belt, black purse, neutral hose or a gray solid or fancy pair of socks and black closed toe pump or a pair of flats

WEEK TWO

Monday
Gray solid skirted suit, white and burgundy multi colored graph check blouse, burgundy belt (optional), burgundy purse, neutral hose and a burgundy closed toe pump

Tuesday
Navy suit jacket or separate blazer, taupe solid or fancy weave slack, ecru solid, tone-on-tone or fancy weave blouse, necklace or strand of pearls, mid tan belt, mid tan purse, neutral hose or a pair of taupe solid or pattern pair of socks and a mid tan closed toe pump or pair of flats

Wednesday
Black stripe skirted suit, white-on-white blouse, necklace or strand of pearls, burgundy belt (optional), neutral hose or a black pattern pair of socks and burgundy closed toe pumps

Thursday
Eggplant solid skirted suit, ivory solid or fancy weave blouse, necklace or strand of pearls, black belt (optional), neutral hose and black closed toe pump

Friday
A black fancy weave sport jacket, black solid or textured weave slack, white fancy weave blouse, black belt, neutral hose or black solid or pattern socks and black closed toe pump or pair of flats

For Saturday and Sunday, visit our Web site at www.DressLikeTheBigFish.com

Example of a
Women's Professional Wardrobe

- ☐ 1 - black solid suit with a skirt
- ☐ 1 - navy solid suit with a skirt
- ☐ 1 - charcoal solid suit with a skirt
- ☐ 1 - black stripe suit with a skirt
- ☐ 1 - charcoal stripe suit with a skirt
- ☐ 1 - taupe solid or fancy weave suit with a skirt
- ☐ 1 - eggplant solid suit with a skirt
- ☐ 4 - white blouses
- ☐ 1 - blue blouse
- ☐ 1 - ink blue end-on-end weave blouse
- ☐ 1 - pink or rose solid or fancy blouse
- ☐ 1 - white and black stripe blouse
- ☐ 1 - white and red stripe blouse
- ☐ 1 - white crew-neck top
- ☐ 1 - ivory crew-neck top
- ☐ 1 - black purse
- ☐ 1 - black belt
- ☐ 2 - pair of black pumps
- ☐ 4 - pair of neutral hose

Example of a
Women's Business Casual Wardrobe

- ☐ 1 - black solid blazer
- ☐ 1 - navy solid blazer
- ☐ 1 - black solid slack
- ☐ 1 - navy solid slack
- ☐ 1 - taupe solid slack
- ☐ 1 - charcoal solid or fancy weave slack
- ☐ 1 - white crew solid top
- ☐ 1 - ivory crew solid top
- ☐ 1 - blue, pink or rose crew solid or fancy top
- ☐ 2 - white solid or fancy blouses
- ☐ 1 - blue solid or end-on-end blouse
- ☐ 1 - ink blue solid or end-on-end blouse
- ☐ 1 - black belt
- ☐ 1 - mid-tan belt
- ☐ 1 - black closed toe pump or loafer
- ☐ 1 - mid-tan closed toe pump or loafer
- ☐ 1 - black, navy and mid-tan purse
- ☐ 2 - pair of slack length black solid or fancy cotton lisle socks
- ☐ 2 - pair of slack length navy solid or fancy cotton lisle socks
- ☐ 1 - pair of slack length charcoal solid or fancy cotton lisle socks
- ☐ 2 - pair of neutral hose

Example of a
Women's Casual Wardrobe

☐ 1 - black solid cotton or microfiber slacks

☐ 1 - black solid or fancy wool slack

☐ 1 - charcoal solid or fancy wool or microfiber slack

☐ 1 - tan solid cotton or microfiber slack

☐ 1 - taupe solid or fancy wool slack

☐ 1 - chino cotton or microfiber slack

☐ 1 - white solid or fancy weave blouse

☐ 1 - blue solid, end-on-end, check or stripe blouse

☐ 1 - ink blue solid or end-on-end weave blouse

☐ 1 - ecru solid, pattern or stripe blouse

☐ 1 - pink or rose solid, pattern or stripe blouse

☐ 1 - melon solid or pattern blouse

☐ 1 - white short-sleeve crew or keyhole top

☐ 1 - pink, ivory, stone, navy or black short sleeve
       crew or keyhole top

☐ 1 - white, pink, rose, black or ivory short sleeve
       cotton polo

☐ 2 - black pair of closed toe low heel pumps or loafers

☐ 1 - mid-tan pair of closed toe low heel pumps or loafers

☐ 2 - pair of black slack length solid or pattern cotton
       lisle socks

☐ 1 - pair of charcoal slack length solid or pattern cotton
       lisle socks

☐ 1 - pair of taupe slack length solid or pattern
       cotton lisle socks

☐ 1 - pair of light tan slack length solid or pattern
       cotton lisle socks

☐ 3 - pair of neutral hose

In summary, these wardrobe examples show some of the many items you can use to build your wardrobe. It takes time to build, it doesn't happen overnight. The intention is not to see how much you can possibly spend.

You want to get enough clothing to mix-and-match so it doesn't look like you are wearing the same outfits over and over again. Build your wardrobe with quality apparel that will last longer. Once you start work or are already working, no matter the type of dress required for work, you want to eventually have enough to get you through a two-week rotation.

Now you know what to do and how to do it. All the material in this book is your guide and is designed to make you a well-informed consumer.

20

Wardrobe Planning

The challenges of my professional life have taken off in the last five years; and as they have done so, the demands on my wardrobe have risen dramatically. With Bel Air Fashions expertise on dress and image, I have experienced a confidence that has permitted me to focus my attention where it ought to be.

– Terry Clark, Professor, Creighton University

Success? Failure? Success is wardrobe planning. Failure is to plan at all. It's like being a fish who's out of water and doesn't know it! You need to examine all aspects of your life, daily routine, places you go, people you see. You have to be able to dress up or down, be consistent with your appearance – all in short order.

If you are going through interviews for a new job and want a good paying career, you need to prepare well. Dress and appearance may be the deciding factor in the hiring decision.

Are you ready, did you plan well? Do you know the required dress for the interview? Do you know the corporate culture?

Wherever your professional career takes you, your planning and attention to details will pay off many times over.

You understand where your needs lie and you plan your clothing purchases accordingly and eliminate apparel that has no place in your wardrobe. In the end you spend less and have clothing that will mix-and-match; you can dress up or down and be ready for any unexpected meeting or client.

Your wardrobe needs to permit you to do this on a year-round basis, whether you are working, traveling on business, or representing your company at a convention or business meeting.

I mention this again and emphasize the point because this serves as your compass. You need to know what you have in your wardrobe, what will mix-and-match and what won't, and then record the items you don't have. Once you know the pieces you need to add to your wardrobe, you can make planned purchases that will work.

If you have a closet full of clothing and nothing to wear or don't have items that will mix-and-match, then you have wasted dollars that give you no return on your investment. Use wardrobe planning. You will see a return on investment. No matter what comes up, you are ready for any situation – from professional to casual to island resort. The true cost of your wardrobe pays off when you buy the right clothing that you can wear year-round. Your garments are made of good fabrics, have quality construction, fit and last a long time and will mix-and-match with your wardrobe.

Planned purchases transition you from a full closet of nothing to wear to fewer clothes that you are able to use all year long.

If you are not sure what goes with what, have someone help you coordinate your clothing, put letters or numbers to each garment, write down the pieces identified with a number or letter, make a spreadsheet.

Put the spreadsheet on your dresser or on the wall in the closet. Then when you need to coordinate an outfit together, you have it.

We have provided such tools for years to our clients. Our clients, who did not know a thing about how to put outfits together, today do a great job at it. Once you keep track and do it repeatedly, it starts to be second nature.

How You Can Be the Big Fish

Buying clothing is not about the label; it is about you, what you do daily and what clothing is going to help you be successful in your dress and appearance. It is not about how much you buy, but buying what you need and being able to wear it year-round.

It's defining you and your image, with an emphasis on your face and message, your clothing is silent, not distracting (90% on your face and less than 10% on your body).

You have a choice. You can be a fish like all the rest in the water or you can separate yourself and be the Big Fish that is noticed.

For simple tools to help you plan a complete, cost-effective wardrobe, visit www.DressLikeTheBigFish.com

RESOURCES

Mehrabian, Albert, Ph.D. *Nonverbal Communication*. Edison,
New Jersey: Aldine Transaction, 2007.

Pease, Allan and Barbara Pease. *The Definitive Book of Body Language*.
New York, New York: Bantam, 2006.

Wainright, Gordon. *Teach Yourself Body Language*. Columbus, Ohio:
McGraw-Hill, 2003.

Glossary

Acrylic – A manufactured fiber in which the fiber-forming substance is any long chain synthetic polymer composed of at least 85% by weight of acrylonitrile units.

Barathea – Usually a twilled hopsack weave – with a fine textured, slightly pebbled surface. (Source: Rotaliana Textiles – Trento, Italy – www.paoli.it)

Bedford Cord – Strong ribbed weave fabric with raised lines or cords produced by warp stuffing threads. May be wool, silk, cotton, etc. Fabric originated in New Bedford, Mass.; hence its name.

Bengaline – Cross-rib material with filling yarn coarser than warp. Made of silk and wool. Wears and drapes well, pronounced filling cords add to the appeal of the cloth.

Birdseye – Fabric with a surface texture of small, uniform spots that suggests a birds eye. (Source: Rotaliana Textiles)

Boucle – Looped-yarn giving a "ring appearance" to the face of the cloth.

Cashmere – The finest Cashmere goat is raised in Tibet – see chapter 6 for complete information on this fabric.

Chambray – Plain-weave, smooth lustrous fabric made of dyed warp and white filling.

Chenille – A cotton, wool, silk, or rayon yarn which has a pile protruding all around at right angles; simulates a caterpillar. After weaving, the fabric is cut between the bunches of warps, and the latter twisted, thereby forming the chenille effect.

Cheviot – Rough woolen suiting and overcoating cloth. Similar to tweed in construction. Name is derived from the fact that hardy wool from Cheviot Hills of Scotland in used in making the cloth.

Chino – A cotton fabric with a plain or twill weave made popular as summer wear for the armed forces.

Color Fastness – The determination as to whether a color is fast in a number of standard tests used for the purpose. Yarn or fabric may be tested for fastness to color fading, with dry cleaning, laundering, sunlight, perspiration, and ironing.

Corduroy – A cut-filling-pile fabric made of cotton, which has hardwearing qualities. When woven with a plain weave back, the fabric is called "tabby-back" corduroy and, when woven with a twill weave back, is known as "genoa-back" corduroy. Corduroy is woven in about the same way as velvet, except that the pile filling picks are bound by the warp yarns to form straight lines of floats, thus producing the ribbed surface. The material is often waxed and singed to remove any long protruding fibers. Corduroy is made with the filling forming the pile effect after the cutting, which is a separate process after the cut of cloth has been taken from the loom.

Covert – Twill usually made of woolen or worsted yarn with two shades of color such as a medium and a light brown. It is a highly desirable cloth and gives smart appearance to the wearer.

Crepe – Characterized by a crinkling surface obtained either by use of (1) hard twist yarns, (2) chemical treatment, (3) weave, (4) embossing.

Dobby – Woven on a dobby loom. Includes material with small figures such as dots, geometrical designs, and floral patterns woven in the fabric.

Donegal – A tweed fabric with thick colored slubs or nubs. (Source: Rotaliana Textiles, Trento, Italy, www.paoli.it/eng/azienda/azienda.htm)

Douppioni – Silk thread from two cocoons that have nested together. In spinning, the double thread is not separated. The yarn is uneven, irregular and large in diameter. It is used in cloth of this name as well as in pongee, nankeen, shantung, etc.

Egyptian Cotton – strong, fine, long and lustrous fibers. (Source: Rotaliana Textiles, Trento, Italy, www.paoli.it)

End-on-End Warp – A warp made from two warps by taking the ends from each warp in an alternating order when the warp dressing is done.

Faille – Ribbed wool, silk or rayon cloth with crosswise rib effect. Good draping effects and wears well.

Flannel – A loosely woven cloth of simple weave, which the dull finish tends to conceal.

Gabardine – A 45- or 63-degree twill. These weaves give the characteristic single-diagonal lines noted on the face of the cloth. Because of the twist in the yarn and texture, the cloth wears very well and outlasts similar materials used for the same purpose.

Glen Plaid – According to the trade interpretation, this is a 4-and-4 and 2-and-2 color effect weave in both warp and filling directions.

Harris Tweed – A trademark for imported tweed made of virgin wool from the Highlands of Scotland. Spun, dyed and hand woven by islanders in Harris and other islands of the Hebrides.

Herringbone – A broken twill weave giving a zigzag effect produced by alternating the direction of the twill. Same as the chevron weave. Structural design resembles backbone of herring.

High Twist – refers to yarns that are manufactured with a relatively high number of turns per inch. This maybe done to increase yarn strength or give the fabric a crepey texture or hand. (Source: Rotaliana Textiles, Trento, Italy, www.paoli.it)

Hopsack – Popular woolen or worsted suiting fabric made from a 2-and-2 or a 3-and-3 basket weave.

Interfacing – Woven or not woven fabrics used between outer fabric and lining to reinforce or stiffen. Some major types include fusible and non-fusible, non-woven, canvas, haircloth.

Linen – Linen is woven from fibers produced by the flax plant, and the term *linen* cannot be applied to any other kind of fiber except that of natural flax. Among the properties of linen are rapid moisture absorption, fiber length of a few inches to one yard, no fuzziness, does not soil quickly, a natural lustre and stiffness.

Lycra – The elastic fiber made by DuPont.

Mercerizing – Treatment for cotton yarns and cotton goods to increase lustre and improve strength and dye affinity.

Merino – A fine, soft yarn made from this wool, often mixed with cotton

Microfiber – Half of the thickness of silk and 100 times finer than a human hair. A microfiber is the tiniest synthetic fiber ever created. Fabrics made of microfiber are wrinkle-resistant and easy care.

Micron (Or Micrometer) – A unit of length, the thousandth part of one millimeter, or the millionth of a meter. This is the unit of measurement employed to designate fiber thickness. One micron is about one twenty-five-thousandth of an inch or, expressing it another way, about forty millionths of an inch. (0.000039 in).

Pic-n-Pic – See End-on-End warp and Sharkskin – tightly woven fabric made of alternative warp and fill threads.

Pima Cotton – Extra-long staple cotton – luxurious feel and strength of the fiber (Source: www.Supimacotton.org).

Pique – Cotton cloth with raised cords that run in the warp direction.

Plain Weave – The simplest, most important and most used of all the hundreds of weaves in the making of textiles. Over 70% of all cloths made each year are made on this simple construction. There is only one plain weave, and it gives a checkerboard appearance. It is made, and repeats, on two warp ends and two filling picks, and is read as "1-up-and-1-down."

Polyester – A manufactured fiber in which the fiber-forming substance is any long chain synthetic polymer composed of at least 85% by weight of an ester of a dihydric alcohol and terephthalic acid.

Polynosic – A high-modulus, dimensionally stable rayon staple fiber. Finer quality than the regular rayon yarns, has high resistance to stretching under wet conditions. Used blended with other yarns in modern and sophisticated fabrics.

Poplin – A broad term applied to several fabrics made from various types of yarn. It is identified by a fine rib effect in the filling direction from selvage to selvage. Plain weave used with rib effect made by the use of warp yarn much finer than filling yarn with a texture or count of two or three times as many ends and picks in the goods.

Rayon – A manufactured fiber composed of regenerated cellulose in which substituents have replaced no more than 15% of hydrogens of the hydroxyl groups.

Saxony – Cloth made of very high-grade wool raised in Saxony, Germany. The name is also applied to soft-finished woolen fabrics of similar fine stock, in fancy yarn effects in the order of tweeds.

Serge – Popular staple, diagonal worsted cloth.

Shantung – Low in lustre, heavy and rough feeling. A plain weave silk in which large irregular filling yarns are used. Also made from several major fibers.

Sharkskin – A fine worsted quality fabric made from small color effect weaves or fancy designs, in which the effect noted in the finished cloth resembles the skin of a shark.

Shetland – (1) A suiting fabric made wholly or partly of shetland wool. The cloth has a raised finish and a rather soft handle. Very popular for suiting and sports wear. (2) A soft knitted fabric made of Shetland wool. (3) Loosely applied to various soft-woven or knits.

Silk – The end product of silk moths. The only natural fiber that comes in a filament form; from 300 to 1,600 yards in length as reeled from the cocoon, cultivated or wild.

Sponging – A pre-shrinkage by dampening with a sponge, by rolling in moist muslin or by steaming, given to woolens and worsted by the cloth maker before cutting to insure against a contraction of the material in the garment. A popular sponging treatment is "London Shrunk," a cold water treatment, originating abroad that is frequently applied and guaranteed by the cloth manufacturers themselves.

Supima – Trademark for a superior type of extra long staple fiber, 1¾" and longer. This is exceptionally high-quality American-Egyptian cotton grown in the southwestern part of the USA.

Striated – Fabric purposely given a narrow, linear, streaked color effect (Rotaliana Textiles, Trento, Italy, www.paoli.it/eng/azienda/azienda.htm)

Staple – Cotton fiber considered with regard to its length and fineness (Source: www.cotton-net.com).

Tear Strength – The force necessary to tear a fabric, usually expressed in pounds or grams.

Tenacity – The breaking strength of fiber, filament, yarn, cord expressed in force per unit yarn number.

Tencel – A miraculous new fiber from the wood pulp of specially selected trees that are grown on agriculturally poor land and are constantly replenished, so there is no threat to the environment. Tencel was introduced to the world of apparel in 1992 and is the first new fiber introduction in over thirty years. Tencel gives fabrics great color richness, from pale pastels to deep vibrant tones. It also has a subtle lustre found only in luxurious fabrics. Comfort and strength are two more properties of Tencel. Strength means high wash stability, extremely low shrinkage and good tear resistance.

Tricotine – A fine quality cavalry twill.

Tropical – Lightweight fabrics used for warm weather wear. They have a clear finish, and high-twist yarns are used to make up for the lack of weight and to provide good performance to consumers.

Tussah – Name of wild silk raised anywhere in the world. Compared with cultivated or true silk, it is more uneven, coarser and stronger. Difficult to dye or bleach.

Tweed – A rough, irregular, soft and flexible, unfinished shaggy woolen named for the Tweed River, which separates England from Scotland. It is made of a two-and-two twill weave, right-hand or left-hand in structure. Outstanding tweeds include Bannockburn, English, Harris, Irish, Linton, Manx, Scotch and Donegal.

Twill Weave – Identified by the diagonal lines in the goods. It is one of the three basic weaves, the others being plain and satin. Most twills are 45 degrees in angle. Steep twills are made from angles of 63, 70, and 75 degrees while reclining twills use angles of 27, 20 and 15 degrees.

Upland Cotton – The largest part of the world's cotton crop is of the Upland type. It is also used as the standard with which other cotton types are compared.

Velour – Thick bodied, close napped, soft type of cloth.

Viscose – See rayon.

Wale – In a knit fabric, the wale is the series of loops, formed by one needle, which runs lengthwise in the material. In a woven fabric, like corduroy or Bedford cord, the wale is the rib or raised cord which runs lengthwise with the warp.

Worsted – A wide range of fabrics is made from worsted yarn and is compactly made from smooth, uniform, well-twisted yarns.

Yarn – A generic term for an assemblage of fibers or filaments, either natural or manufactured, twisted together to form a continuous strand that can be used for weaving, knitting.

Sources:
Rotaliana Textiles, Trento, Italy,
    www.paoli.it/eng/azienda/azienda.htm
www.SupimaCotton.org
www.cotton-net.com
Ballin of Canada, makers of fine men's slacks, www.ballin.com

Index

About the Author

A lifelong Omaha resident, author Dick Lerner, CWC, CCC, along with his brother Sheldon have been in the clothing business since they were young boys. Working in the family clothing business run by their father, Joseph, and grandfather, Max, the boys gained a wealth of knowledge and experience that has served them well throughout their careers.

Dick Lerner holds a degree in business from the University of Nebraska–Lincoln, and after graduation started working full-time in the family business in 1973. His learning never stopped.

He completed professional programs at Haas Tailoring to become a Certified Custom Clothier and attended the prestigious Haggar Institute at the A. B. Freeman School of Business at Tulane University in New Orleans. He later completed coursework offered by the Men's Retail Association to become a Certified Wardrobe Consultant – a program conducted by the Wichita State University School of Business and another at the Philadelphia School of Textiles and Science.

Lerner starting conducting workshops over 33 years ago to assist men and women in choosing their working wardrobes. He has never stopped the teaching process. He works extensively in transitioning military men and women into civilian careers (and into appropriate clothing). He has also conducted workshops for students in high school and universities, and for businesses and organizations. He and his brother are grateful to the many loyal clients (some celebrities too) who have allowed them to help in wardrobe planning.

As Lerner says, "Our premise has always been that nobody is going to open up your garment to see what label you are wearing! The important part is on the outside. What you wear helps define your image and abilities. We always feel as if we are clothing doctors.

We need to get enough information about our client's day-to-day activities to make sure their wardrobe meets their needs."

They say that fit is about fine tuning and sweating the small details. A wardrobe, done right, makes a powerful statement about someone's image and appearance.

LaVergne, TN USA
09 February 2011
215765LV00002B/2/P